SYLVANDIRE

Borgo Press Books by ALEXANDRE DUMAS

Anthony
The Count of Monte Cristo, Part One: The Betrayal of Edmond Dantès
The Count of Monte Cristo, Part Two: The Resurrection of Edmond Dantès
The Count of Monte Cristo, Part Three: The Rise of Monte Cristo
The Count of Monte Cristo, Part Four: The Revenge of Monte Cristo
A Fairy Tale (with Adolphe de Leuven and Léon Lhérie)
The Last of the Three Musketeers; or, The Prisoner of the Bastille (Musketeers #3)
The Three Musketeers—Twenty Years Later (Musketeers #2)
Napoléon Bonaparte
Richard Darlington
The San Felice
Sylvandire
The Three Musketeers (Musketeers #1)
The Two Dianas
Urbain Grandier and the Devils of Loudon
The Venetian
The Whites and the Blues
Young Louix XIV

RELATED DRAMAS:

The Queen's Necklace, by Pierre Decourcelle
The Son of Porthos the Musketeer, by Émile Blavet (Musketeers #4)
A Summer Night's Dream, by Adolphe de Leuven and Joseph-Bernard Rosier
The Widow's Husband; and, Porthos in Search of an Outfit: Two Dumasian Comedies (Frank J. Morlock, editor)

SYLVANDIRE
A PLAY IN FOUR ACTS

ALEXANDRE DUMAS

Translated and Adapted by Frank J. Morlock

THE BORGO PRESS
MMXII

SYLVANDIRE

Copyright © 2001, 2012 by Frank J. Morlock

FIRST BORGO PRESS EDITION

Published by Wildside Press LLC

www.wildsidebooks.com

DEDICATION

For John Cordell

Great Friend, Great Chef

CONTENTS

CAST OF CHARACTERS 9
ACT I 11
ACT II 56
ACT III 98
ACT IV 151
ABOUT THE AUTHOR 193

CAST OF CHARACTERS

CHEVALIER ROGER D'ANGUILHEM

MR. DE VILLIERS, Farmer-General

VICOMTE D'HERBIGNY, Naval Officer

AFGHANO, a right Indian

FINARD, go-between and man of affairs

TOURANGEAU, Roger's Servant

BASQUE, a servant

MULEI-BEN-OMAR, a pirate captain

A CLERK

A SAILOR

MISS POUSETTE, a dancer at the Opera

SYLVANDIRE

FINETTE, Sylvandire's chambermaid

A CLERK (played by a woman)

GUESTS, PASSENGERS, SAILORS, ETC.

ACT I

The Hotel of the Marquis de Crette, Paris. A small, very elegant salon in Louis XV style.

At rise, d'Herbigny and Mlle Pousette de Villiers are at table at the right, surrounded by valet serving them.

CHORUS

What a pleasure
What a delicious meal
In these parts—
Pleasure serves us
Pleasure serves you
Pleasure serves them
Exquisite wines—
Happy words
Lovely Lady
Each in turn
Charm us
Charm you
Charm them

D'HERBIGNY

I propose the first toast to the health of Miss Pousette—to our ravishing hostess.

DE VILLIERS

The most charming Hindu dancing girl of the Opera.

POUSETTE

Not at all, gentlemen—nothing could be more unjust. The first toast to the brave, generous Marquis de Crette—gallant lord who left on his embassy—placing at my disposal his brilliant hotel—and ordering me to receive and entertain his good friends—you, especially Vicomte d'Herbigny, his faithful friend, and you, Mr. de Villiers—the richest and most honest financier who has flourished in tax farming and salt taxes.

ALL THREE

(glasses in hand)

To the Marquis de Crette.

DE VILLIERS

Who has ordered us to console you.

POUSETTE

Who told you I am sad?

DE VILLIERS

But it seems to me that the absence of the beloved object—

POUSETTE

To our health, my little Cupids—but until now, there's never been a man who could boast of having prevented Pousette from laughing and singing from morning until evening—that astonishes you? Well—(pointing to her heart)—there's still nothing therefore anyone—no more for Crette than for any other—He was rich, he was handsome, he paid court to me—that's true—but, word of honor, word of Pousette—there's nothing more than good friendship in our relationship—you see, Vicomte, I'm searching for a passion—a real love, something that will make me very unhappy—find that for me, kids, you will be pleasing me greatly.

D'HERBIGNY

Now there's an idea!

DE VILLIERS

Come, come my darling—you are spinning tales for us out of the air and but for the Opera, you must have—

POUSETTE

For the Opera! Fie! Do you take me for a Duchess? I don't come from glitter and finery, my jewel—I don't love people it's true—but even so, they must please me before I permit them to love me—

DE VILLIERS

Yes, and for them to please you, they must have at least 50,000 a year in income.

POUSETTE

Well, there again, you are mistaken, great financier and my friend—and the proof is that the other day I gave an Indian Prince his walking papers—who put 500,000 pounds at my feet—only that.

D'HERBIGNY

Plague—now there's a savage seems to me to really have the air of knowing how to live.

POUSETTE

He wasn't handsome, it's true—but he was curious looking—yellow like a lemon, a real quince on the shoulders of a man and I know more than one of my good lady friends would have listened to him if only to know how a declaration of love is made in Malabar.

DE VILLIERS

And what name does your Indian answer to?

POUSETTE

To the name Afghano.

D'HERBIGNY

Plague! He bears a name that is not common.

DE VILLIERS

You still should have accepted the half million—fool that you are.

POUSETTE

Yes—but the half-million and the good man of gingerbread don't without each other.

BASQUE

(entering from the back) Madame, a waiter who is old enough, ugly enough—half peasant, half house servant demands earnestly to deliver a litter to the Marquis de Crette.

D'HERBIGNY

Some annoying person—let him go to the devil.

POUSETTE

One moment, one moment gentlemen—I order in the hotel of the Marquis—I replace the Marquis here, it may involve some important business for Crette.

(to Basque) Let this boy come in right away—

(to others) If there is a good action to perform, he wouldn't forgive me for having failed to do it.

(Basque makes a sign at the back, and Tourangeau appears in the aged livery of a provincial household servant—he dries his feet then comes forward, bowing. Basque leaves.)

TOURANGEAU

Good day to you all, gentlemen and lady—how is everybody.

ALL

(laughing) Ha! Ha! Ha!—Excellent.

POUSETTE

(laughing) Why, well enough, my lad—as you see.

TOURANGEAU

Indeed, you don't seem to me to engender melancholy

and you break bread very gracefully—

DE VILLIERS

From where did this character fall to us?

TOURANGEAU

First of all, I didn't fall, I came—

DE VILLIERS

Well, then—from where do you come?

TOURANGEAU

Ah! My God—quite simply from Chinon—

(aside) They seem to me to be guys who love to laugh; I am going to laugh with them; that will put them at their ease with me right off.

D'HERBIGNY

What's Chinon?

POUSETTE

(laughing) By God—it's the capital of Japan.

TOURANGEAU

(warming up) You don't know Chinon! You don't know

Chinon! My dear, gentlemen, I am afflicted to tell you so publicly but that does little honor toy our studies in geography. Chinon is an old town on the Vienne, which possesses a Château—castle and several convents—where they make dried plums as good as those of Tours—whatever jealousy and ill will may say about it.

(aside) I slipped this to hear in passing without having seemed to say anything.

POUSETTE

You are a patriotic lad—you love your country—that's something already—well, look, what is it you want?

TOURANGEAU

(looking at them) Damn—I ask which of these gentlemen is the Marquis de Crette?

POUSETTE

(seriously) That's me.

(They raise the table—servants bring forward a round table and bring coffee and liqueurs.)

TOURANGEAU

Huh? Ah, bah! You! Come off it—this is a fame—your sex is naturally opposed to your being a man—at most you maybe a Marquise—later, you will tell me in Paris you see so many extraordinary things.

POUSETTE

And what do you want with the Marquis de Crette?

TOURANGEAU

To deliver to his own hand this letter addressed to him.

POUSETTE

(taking the letter) Give it here.

(perusing it) Eh! Eh! Milords—it's from the Chevalier Roger d'Anguilhem, son of an intimate friend of Crette's father who asks to present himself at the home of the Marquis—about a pressing affair.

D'HERBIGNY

A little Squireen who is coming to solicit some office at the Court and who sends his Herald from fifty leagues.

POUSETTE

However, that may be gentlemen, I cannot show him the door.

(to Tourangeau) What's your name, Buffoon?

POUSETTE

And what sort of man is he?

TOURANGEAU

Oh—a superb man—taller than me by this—and in other respects—manufactured like these gents—it's not for me to do him honor, but if you were to see him in his green dress that his mother had made for him at Blois—I would dare say the sight would agreeably flatter you.

POUSETTE

Really—he has a green dress?

DE VILLIERS

It's of the latest fashion.

D'HERBIGNY

Well, there's your affairs, Pousette. You were searching for a passion.

TOURANGEAU

Ah, I am distressed about it, you've come too late. The place is taken.

POUSETTE

(laughing) Ah—he has a lover.

TOURANGEAU

I think so indeed! And who bears a promising name—Miss Constance.

DE VILLIERS

Constance what?

TOURANGEAU

Constance de Benzerie—it's one of the best in Touraine—do you know that the Baron de Benzerie has a great forest which he can pass on to the head of his son-in-law?—not counting the great Prairie of La Pintade, which alone in Lucerne will put pretty good hay in his barns.

POUSETTE

That's fine, my friend—return to your Chevalier—and tell him he can come—and that we are impatient to make his acquaintance.

TOURANGEAU

With pleasure, Madame le Marquis—much better that we are living opposite the Golden Harrow—an inn very well inhabited—all wool merchants from Berry and big horse dealers from Poitou.

D'HERBIGNY

And when did you get here—?

TOURANGEAU

Since day before yesterday.

D'HERBIGNY

By the coach?

TOURANGEAU

Come on! That's good for nurses—we came with Christophe a magnificent stallion which yesterday they offered to buy from my master for fifteen shillings.

POUSETTE

Go! Go! We are in a hurry to see him.

TOURANGEAU

Christophe?

POUSETTE

No—your master.

D'HERBIGNY

Go quickly then, beast!

TOURANGEAU

I am running.

(aside) What exquisite politeness in the French Court.

(he leaves)

D'HERBIGNY

Hooray! This is a good fortune, which falls on us from heaven—I am keeping the provincial—I ask only that he be loaned to me; I will monopolize him to my profit—now here's an opportunity to spend time discovered.

DE VILLIERS

Easy, easy gentlemen—don't go too far—think that this poor gentlemen is here under my protection and don't compromise the name of Crette.

D'HERBIGNY

Spare us your mortality and since you don't permit us the least little liberties, abandon to us, at least for our humble pleasures, the little squireen who falls into our hands.

(The door at the back opens.)

BASQUE

(announcing) Chevalier Roger Tancred d'Anguilhem.

ALL

Ah.

DE VILLIERS

I am going to hang on his neck.

D'HERBIGNY

I want to persuade him, he is my cousin.

POUSETTE

(gesturing) Hush! Hush.

(D'Herbigny and de Villiers go to the round table—servants serve coffee.)

ROGER

(enters dressed quite simply, but there is nothing ridiculous about him) Good God, Madame, I ask a million pardons for coming at such a bad time to present myself to you—would you, I beg you, be so good as to indicate to me your hour of receiving, and I shall have the honor of returning.

POUSETTE

(looking at him with surprise) Not at all, sir—and since you are here—be welcome.

ROGER

That's too kind!

(low to Tourangeau) But I don't see the Marquis.

TOURANGEAU

(pointing to Pousette) There—there—

ROGER

(pushing him away) Get out, imbecile.

POUSETTE

The Marquis de Crette is absent, Chevalier, but I replace him—would you then employ me and dispose of my good will to be agreeable to you.

ROGER

The offer is so obliging; Madame—that one cannot help being a bit embarrassed.

DE VILLIERS

(low to d'Herbigny) Why, this young man isn't stupid at all.

POUSETTE

(low to d'Herbigny) He's not bad to look at either.

ROGER

(noting with what curiosity they are looking at him) You must pardon me a little clumsiness, Madame, I can see all your indulgence in your eyes—and I know I have great need of it—

(the others look at him favorably) Oh—one must be frank—I am only a poor provincial, really ridiculous, I feel it—and very annoying perhaps—for I've never left Anguilhem—but there's a well-placed heart under a simple dress and I will know, I swear to you, how to be grateful for your gracious greeting.

D'HERBIGNY

(low to de Villiers) Why that is fine—he talks well—decidedly Touraine is beginning to be part of France.

DE VILLIERS

(low) What do you want me to say—we've been robbed.

POUSETTE

(with great alacrity) And what good wind brings you to Paris, Mr. d'Anguilhem?

ROGER

(gaily and putting himself at his ease) Alas, beautiful lady, I don't know much if it can be called a good wind—for it's a piece of chicanery. I am coming for a trial.

DE VILLIERS

(a cup of coffee in his hand) Ah! They litigate in Chinon too—? That must be amusing—a provincial lawsuit. It's a question of a party wall no doubt?

ROGER

No, sir—rather an inheritance of 1,500 thousand pounds they are contesting with me.

DE VILLIERS

1,500 thousand pounds! Plague! That's a very pretty little sum.

D'HERBIGNY

(glass in hand) I drink to the 1,500 thousand pounds of the Chevalier d'Anguilhem.

ROGER

One moment—they are not yet in my pocket! The Devil! Don't go so fast.

D'HERBIGNY

(raising his glass) To the beautiful Constance de Benzerie, the Pearl of Touraine.

ROGER

Bah—you know—

(looking at Tourangeau) Ah! My imbecile already told that with his sacristan's tongue?

(gaily) All the same, he's not so bad. Paris God, gentlemen and not to confess the lady is a cowardice.

(sings) If we were in times of gallantry, I would maintain my lady outstrips all other women with her marvelous allures and the charm in her eyes—I would boast of her lovable grace; her unchangeable heart—I'd say she was incomparable.

(bowing to Pousette) If Madame was not here.

POUSETTE

(to herself) Why, he's charming—this dear Chevalier. I am already mad about him.

(The servants clean up and leave.)

D'HERBIGNY

By God, my friend we are only churls if we don't help Milord Roger Tancred d'Anguilhem win his lawsuit.

ROGER

Eh, eh, gentleman don't commit yourselves too deeply—the thing is hard to bring off—I have, I warn you, a tough case—I inherit directly from the Vicomte de Bouzenois, my mother's brother—dead without children—but imagine a circumstance which my father and I were not expecting—I find in my path a character—an Indian name Afghano whose mother my respectable uncle had married—on the left hand.

ALL

Afghano!

POUSETTE

My lemon! I'll take care of him—and he'll leave for Madagascar with no more than lemon peel.

D'HERBIGNY

We shall do our utmost.

ROGER

Truly, my dear sirs, you see me filled with gratitude and admiration! I confess to you I was not expecting so much goodwill towards me, a stranger in this great city—me, a poor devil of a country boy who will see myself reduced to entering the King's service and renouncing my loves if I lose my case. Therefore, receive my sincere thanks—and as I fear to disturb you by staying much longer—allow me to take leave of you.

POUSETTE

(excitedly) What do you mean take leave? Why, not at all—Chevalier. If Crette was here, he wouldn't hear of it and it would be an insult to me to leave this hotel—I am keeping you, I am protecting you—! By Jove, it would be strange if a handsome gentleman like you—who's expecting an inheritance of 1,500 thousand pounds were to be lodged in the Golden Harrow when he has Mr. Crette as a friend and Miss Pousette for a protectress!

ROGER

(surprised) Miss Pousette.

POUSETTE

That's my name. As for my profession I am a girl from

the Opera as they say—

TOURANGEAU

(aside) Ah, for me, I really knew that she wasn't the Marquise.

POUSETTE

But a good sort of a girl—you will see—so you'll remain, you'll live here—that's agreed—you, your people and your baggage.

TOURANGEAU

(drunk with joy) Christophe and I—we accept!

ROGER

Oh! Madame—truly you overwhelm me.

POUSETTE

And first of all, Chevalier, pardon what I am going to say to you but you must get rid of this traveling outfit which does not become an heir of your appearance.

(calling) Hola! Basque! Rameau—Baspole.

(Three servants enter by the back.)

POUSETTE

Have someone run right away to the Marquis' tailor—the Marquis' seamstress and the Marquis' hairdresser—

(to Roger) I will take care of decking you out, my pretty—I know about it and you will be pretty as a picture word of a tree nymph.

ROGER

Madame.

POUSETTE

Meanwhile, everything here is at your service—beasts and men.

TOURANGEAU

(gives a gesture of joy)

POUSETTE

Heavens! On the subjects of animals—this child—needs to be metamorphosed also—

(laughing—looking at Tourangeau) God! He's got a funny face—! Come here—let me look at you.

(he approaches—she taps his cheek) I am going to make you my errand boy.

TOURANGEAU

God—she gave me two taps—oh—again! Again!

(he winks grotesquely)

POUSETTE

(to the others) To the rehearsal—"Pyramis and Thesbe reclaims me—I allow all my adorers to follow me"—that's less compromising.

D'HERBIGNY

(offering his hand to her) The hand at least is the only favor permitted me.

POUSETTE

(low to d'Herbigny—pointing to Roger) Ah, Vicomte—that guy has caught my eye—by all the devils I'm afraid of being taken.

TOGETHER

Let's go! The Opera calls me. Always faithful to duty—I must apply myself with fervor—soon—we shall meet again.

ALL

Let's go—the Opera calls me, calls you, calls her.

(Repeat last three lines above.)

POUSETTE

(singing) Courage—handsome Chevalier—I promise to help you—despite the Indian and his fury—you will have your inheritance. Ah—what a shame it would be with this air, this face—to see such a handsome party despoiled by a savage—

TOGETHER

Let's go—

POUSETTE

Soon, my darling, soon!

(They leave.)

ROGER

(astonished) My darling.

TOURANGEAU

My darling, she calls you her darling.

ROGER

What is it you are saying about that? Do you understand anything about it?

TOURANGEAU

Mr. Chevalier, I am looking everywhere to see if I see a sorcerer—I am feeling myself from head to toe to convince myself I am really in my skin and bones—Olympse—Thaneais Tourangeau!

ROGER

Why, it's great luck! It's a blow from heaven—to find immediately at the moment I least expected it friends so devoted, so generous—! Still, truly, I have some scruples. Is it right for me to accept in this way, without manners, the obliging offers they've just made me? The Marquis is absent, and I don't know exactly who Miss Poussette is.

TOURANGEAU

Ah, by God, Mr. Chevalier, Excuse me, but you are making us yawn with your scruples! First of all, Miss Poussette is a charming woman who called you her darling and who has the most distinguished manners—if she invites you, then she has the right—and the bottom line—it's a loan to repay. When you've won your case, when you are swimming in gold and in well becalmed shops—you will return to the Marquis all his kindness—what the devil, between gentlemen it's done like that—it's done like that.

ROGER

Yes—if I win my lawsuit.

TOURANGEAU

Bah! You will win it; I am sure of it now and no later than right away, I am going to seek your valise and my effects at the Golden Harrow, to inform them we are living with our friend the Marquis de Crette—and as Christophe is invited, too—I am taking him forthwith to the stables of his friend and the Marquis de Crette.

ROGER

Do it as you intend, wise guy—after all—it's God's grace!

TOURANGEAU

Wait for me, Chevalier, I am going to have our baggage and wardrobe transported—that won't be long and it especially won't be very heavy.

(he leaves)

ROGER

Come on—let's suppose it's a dream I'm having—the awakening will be cruel—but as I foresee it in advance—the blow will be less rough. Eh, my God! If I was alone in this world what would these 1,500 thousand pounds of Mr. de Benzerie matter to me—without them, I would still have enough to live on so long as a sword remained to me to place in the service of the King. But my poor parents have the whole of their small fortune engaged in this wretched affair—they are not already very rich—and the expenses they will have to pay are going to completely ruin them. Ah—for all my courage, I feel that idea is killing me.

BASQUE

(entering from the rear) Sir—a man with a face not very pleasant—and who stinks of chicanery at three quarters of a league off—asks if he can have the privilege of speaking to you in private.

ROGER

Who is this? Some bawler of the palace? Some miser of Saint Chapelle? Show him in.

(Basque introduces Finard, who enters from the rear with a shy look and waits to come forward until the valet leaves.)

ROGER

(aside) Oh—oh—pleasing face—

FINARD

(very mysteriously) Is it really to the Chevalier Roger

Tancred d'Anguilhem that I have the honor of speaking?

ROGER

To myself—sir—what's it all about?

FINARD

(looking around) Are we really alone, Chevalier?

ROGER

Perfectly alone, sir—as you see!

FINARD

Permit me to make sure.

(going to the door at the right and opening it—looking in)

ROGER

(aside) Now, here's a curious character, for goodness sake!

FINARD

(crossing to the left) You are quite sure no one's hidden in this salon over in the chamber?

(opens the chamber door at the left)

ROGER

(impatiently) By God—everybody having left, I conclude no one's there.

FINARD

(looking under a covered table) Nor under this furniture?

ROGER

(laughing) Sir—here are my two pockets—you can check them, too.

(aside) Could he be some police clerk?

FINARD

I humbly ask your pardon for all these precautions, Chevalier—but you will soon understand they are rigorously necessary.

ROGER

See here, sir, I am listening to you.

FINARD

I had first of all presented myself at the Golden Harrow, but your servant did me the pleasure of informing me that henceforth you were lodging with your friend the

Marquis de Crette.

ROGER

(emphasizing) Yes, sir—I am lodging henceforth at the home of my friend, the Marquis de Crette. Now, come to the point.

FINARD

I almost wish we were seated, Chevalier—isolated thus in the middle of this salon we would be even more certain of not being spied on—

ROGER

(sitting) As you wish, my dear sir—

FINARD

(seated by Roger) Now, Mr. d'Anguilhem, I shall broach the question without preamble.

ROGER

I ask nothing better, I confess—

FINARD

Would you like to win your case?

ROGER

(jumping in his seat) I should say so! And a lot, I swear to you.

FINARD

(empathetically) Well, as for me, sir, I can make you win it.

ROGER

(transported) What do you say? Ah, you are my savior—you are an angel, you are a God—! I would like to embrace you—word of a gentleman.

(aside) If you weren't so ugly—

(aloud) Ah! Speak—explain yourself, man from heaven—what must be done? What must one give? I am ready for any sacrifice.

FINARD

Oh—my God—almost nothing—quite simply—it's a question of you marrying—

ROGER

Me marrying!

FINARD

Or signing provisionally this promise of marriage whose names are in blank, and which is only executory, of course, until after the winning of your case.

ROGER

Very well! Now that's perfectly clear—I have to marry—my God—that's easy to understand—the whole world is prone to it, but marry with whom? You really think, my excellent friend, that I cannot enter a contract of this importance and of this duration playing at—blind man's bluff—

FINARD

Still those are the conditions insisted on Chevalier.

ROGER

What—I have to get married. Without knowing my wife?

FINARD

Precisely.

ROGER

(rising) Come on, this is a bad joke—and if it's a joke, sir—I tell you it displease me and it offends me.

FINARD

If it's a joke Chevalier—your whole future is involved in it—since you can win 1,500 thousand pounds. Consider the business—it's worth the trouble that one put a little of oneself in it.

ROGER

A little of myself—he is sweet! A lot of myself. Look, my tender sir, what's your name?

FINARD

Finard—to serve you.

ROGER

Pretty name—I think it suits you marvelously—look my amiable sir, Mr. Finard—let's see a little bit of information—the young woman—person—is she—you know huh? First of all—is she young?

FINARD

I am forced to remain mute.

ROGER

You are provoking. Tell me at least—is she well made or deformed—girl or widow?

FINARD

All that I can do for you without compromising myself is to allow you time for reflecting.

ROGER

Right! Now that's talking. At least give folks leisure to breathe—one doesn't marry at gunpoint.

FINARD

I give you a quarter of an hour.

ROGER

A quarter of an hour? Now, by Jove, that's a nice business!

FINARD

Ah—damn—we have no time to lose—as you know.

ROGER

Yet one more question—how is it that my future father-in-law hasn't offered his daughter to my adversary—

FINARD

We did offer her—and he almost accepted—but, you see—he's ugly and you're a pretty fellow—and then the name Afghano—that smells of savagery—d'Anguilhem—that sounds better to French ears—in short, we decided to give you preference.

ROGER

I am much obliged to you—and if in a quarter of an hour, I refuse—?

FINARD

In twenty minutes, I am at the home of Mr. Afghano—no goodbyes, Chevalier—

(going) Don't escort me—no ceremonies—no need to awaken attention—1,500 thousand pounds or a little zero for your manor—those are the figures well stated.

(bowing) I am your humble servant—

(he leaves)

ROGER

(alone) Go to the devil, cursed Jew!

(walking about) I shall never consent to such! This ridiculous marriage is impossible. It's a trap that my adversary has set for me—I won't fall into it—these threats prove that my cause is just—and that my adversaries are trembling and trying to frighten me.

(noticing Pousette, who enters) Ah, it's you—

POUSETTE

(singing) Alas, three times alas—my poor Menelaus—

(speaking) How they sing at the Opera—bad news, my dear guest—your case is lost—or it's all.

ROGER

How do you know this?

POUSETTE

I skipped my rehearsal in your honor—I ran to see an influential lawyer friend of mine.

ROGER

Well—?

POUSETTE

It seems that this buffalo from India has won over everybody. The judges are for him. He's given a life annuity to the parrot of an advisor, and given 10,000 crowns worth of diamonds to the monkey of a President. Only the Counselor-Reporter, the incorruptible Bonteau, has refused to see him.

ROGER

And when I think that if I wanted to—despite all that—

POUSETTE

What—despite all that?

ROGER

There's a way for me to win my case.

POUSETTE

(excited) What are you saying?

ROGER

Yes, great things have occurred since your departure, my dear Miss Pousette. A sort of man-fox-monkey left here—he shares three natures—who quite simply proposed to assure me the winning of my case.

POUSETTE

Really?

ROGER

They only asked me for this trifle, this mere nothing; it's simply a question of my marrying in fifteen minutes or what's all the same, singing an engagement, by means of which I will enjoy without sharing—my uncle's inheritance—the Vicomte de Bouzenois and with a woman who is doubtless one-eyed, hump-backed, bandy-legged or possessing some other quality unknown to me—seeing that I am enjoined to take her without knowing her and without seeing her otherwise than with the eyes of faith.

POUSETTE

And by means of this marriage winning the case is assured?

ROGER

Nothing is done without this certainly—the clauses are perfectly drawn—I have a quarter of an hour to decide.

POUSETTE

Marry, Chevalier, marry—with 1,500 thousand pounds in view, you can go there with your eyes shut.

ROGER

But consider that I am in love.

POUSETTE

It's always a folly to be in love but today—it's more than that—it's a stupidity.

ROGER

To think that Constance will marry in her turn.

POUSETTE

All the better for you, my dear—all the better! You won't have it on your conscience—remorse for having made her remain unmarried—to remain a virgin—an old maid—nothing's more stupid than that! At least, she won't be a dancer—

(Finard appears at the back watch in hand looking at it.)

ROGER

(noticing him) Ah, my God! Already.

POUSETTE

What already?

ROGER

(pointing to Finard) The man about the marriage!

(Pousette withdraws to the right.)

FINARD

(entering mysteriously) We have sixteen and a half

minutes—I gave an extra share to the Chevalier—

(noticing Pousette) But the gentleman's not alone, I see and I can only withdraw.

ROGER

No, no—remain—and come hither, obliging, Mr. Finard.

(Finard approaches, Pousette moves quietly to the left) I think he's more of the crocodile than any other sort of animals.

FINARD

Here's the paper in question—Come Chevalier—1,500 thousand pounds for a stroke of the pen.

ROGER

(taking the pen) Give it to me)

(hesitating) Why—no—no—it's impossible!

POUSETTE

(low to Roger) Look, Chevalier, some heart—what the devil! You are forced to take a wife but the engagement doesn't say you are obliged to idolize her.

ROGER

That's all it lacks!

POUSETTE

Well—consider then—ruin or fortune!

ROGER

But—

POUSETTE

Your parents in misery!

ROGER

(making the decision, he goes to sit at the table) Yes, for them—you are right!

POUSETTE

(handing Roger the pen) Sign!

(he hesitates)

ROGER

(signing and hurling the paper at Finard's feet) May the plague choke you—infidel that you are!

FINARD

(picking up the contract that he folds carefully) You couldn't put it more gracefully—thanks, Chevalier—day after tomorrow at noon—a carriage will come to take you and conduct you to your future wife—who the same day will become your wife—

ROGER

(retaining him) But who is this woman in the name of heaven—a word—one single word?

FINARD

Sir—you are doing a magnificent business.

(leaves bowing)

ROGER

(annihilated) So—everything is finished!

POUSETTE

(going to him) Look, my little Chevalier, some philosophy—if your wife is rather too queer-looking—you will put her in a glass jar with 100,000 pounds for her upkeep and with the 1,400 thousand pounds which remain to you—you won't lack consolation—very sweet ones.

(Basque and the Marquis' dressers enter) Heavens—here are all our people coming—look—resign yourself—first of all, you must appear like a handsome and rich gentleman—which you are—I myself are going to preside over your toilet.

ROGER

I am abandoning myself to you, charming Pousette—dress up the victim—so he may be ready for the sacrifice.

(They bring a dressing table from the back.)

POUSETTE

Come—to work—all of you! Powder à la marshal—Pomade à la tubereau—some essence of lily of the valley, let them smarten him up—let them coddle him—let them dress him up—

CHORUS

Hurry—dress him up—let it be finished—
From head to toe—
Do him, you, us—honor—
With that face
Thanks to your/our work—
At Court,
I bet,
He's a sensation.

TOURANGEAU

(entering from the back in a rich errand boy costume) Look out, look out—let me by—

ALL

(laughing) Ha! Ha! Ha!

TOURANGEAU

Here, sir—look how they've taken care of me. I am all ablaze, huh?

ROGER

(who cannot prevent himself from laughing) You are superb, my lad—you are giving me the effect of a fancy valet.

TOURANGEAU

Oh, a valet. A servant of the king of hearts—I don't say!

POUSETTE

(to Roger) Come on—come on—I want you to smell nice, spruce, stunning, astounding—don't interfere, go my darling.

(Roger sits at the table; they surround him and begin

to dress him and do his hair as the Chorus takes up its refrain—

CHORUS

Hurry—dress him up!

(etc.)

CURTAIN

ACT II

A small room. Very simple. Doors at the back and the sides. A window to the right. A table to the left, armchairs, etc.

FINARD

(seated to the left, a clerk standing before him) Listen to me, Mister Wideawake—a carriage with a livery and gold will stop any minute at our door—a handsome gentleman will descend from it.

(heading towards the door at the right—the Clerk follows him) You will discreetly escort him here—by means of this hidden stairway—

(goes to look out the window) No—that's still for that German doctor who established himself on the ground floor—he's announced that he can restore youth and beauty to the most deformed and decrepit woman—so the beautiful sex, that is to say the villainous sex flock to him. But go, Master Wideawake, go—rap three times and I myself will open.

(The Clerk leaves by the right.)

FINARD

Everything's going fine! We will bring it off—my patron will be satisfied—this very day he will richly establish his daughter—and I, as his faithful representative in this affair—I shall not be forgotten—on the other hand, if I can cause the plans of the Marquis of Royancourt to succeed, my fortune is made.

(the door at the back opens) Who's coming there?

(he goes and notices Afghano who cannot yet be seen) The Devil—Afghano! The Indian—our adversary— Let's lock up!

(Afghano enters, bowing.)

FINARD

Your very humble, sir—what can I do to serve you?

AFGHANO

(abruptly) By Jove, sir—you ought, it seems to me to know just as well as I do. I've come to talk of our business.

FINARD

(pretending astonishment) Our business?

AFGHANO

No doubt.

FINARD

I am completely unaware—

AFGHANO

Don't you recognize me?

FINARD

I have never had the honor of seeing you.

AFGHANO

What the devil, sir—we are alone—let's end this joking.

FINARD

You mistake me, sir, I assure you—

AFGHANO

Your face is original enough so one doesn't forget it, if it has been but one time.

FINARD

In that case, sir, I ought to remember yours.

AFGHANO

Look—I repeat to you—we are alone—and we can play cards on the table—you came yesterday to my hotel.

FINARD

Me!

AFGHANO

You! The proposition you made me was extraordinary enough—no matter, I considered—and I accept this proposition—I'll marry—

FINARD

You'll marry who?

AFGHANO

Eh—Dawns! The woman you offered me—the woman who will assure me the winning of my case against the Anguilhems'. I'll marry her blindfolded—bring me to her, let me marry her—and be done with it.

FINARD

Sir, you take me for someone else.

AFGHANO

No, by God! I take you for my own—and here is the earnest money.

(gives him a purse) You will receive double, after the winning of my case against these Anguilhems'.

FINARD

Ah—I think I understand you at least.

AFGHANO

That's really fortunate.

FINARD

You are Mr. Afghano?

AFGHANO

Doubtless.

FINARD

Who the Councilor refused to receive ten times.

AFGHANO

Yes—but for you, I received you yesterday at my place.

FINARD

And you represent yourself—gold in hand to inveigle us, to seduce us.

AFGHANO

From others!

FINARD

To corrupt us!

AFGHANO

Don't shout so loud.

FINARD

This is an infamy!

AFGHANO

Sir!

FINARD

An indignity.

AFGHANO

Yet once more.

FINARD

(going to the door) Leave, sir, leave this very instant.

AFGHANO

Ah, you assume that tone? Well, yes—I am leaving—but I've got my eye on what's happening—for I suspect—

FINARD

Yet once more, leave this honorable dwelling—know that, amongst us, justice is not sold, as in your country—in India, in Malabar—and that all the gold in Peru, all the diamonds in Columbia would not make the scales of justice lean in our hands—goodbye, sir!

AFGHANO

Go to the devil!

(he leaves furious)

FINARD

(laughing) Eh! Eh! Eh! Poor dupe!

(three knocks at the door on the right) Ah—here's our son-in-law—our pretty son-in-law.

(goes to open) Enter, Chevalier, enter—

(Roger enters) Your very humble and very obedient—Mr. d'Anguilhem—I was waiting for you.

ROGER

You see I am precise, sir—

FINARD

Yes, Chevalier, I see that you are an honest gentleman, and if you had trouble deciding, at least when you made your decision, you are acting grandly.

ROGER

Now, sir—will you tell me in whose house I am—? For up to now, I've only seen you—I've known you I've asked only you. This young girl—I say young—this girl that I cannot describe—is she your child, your sister, your niece, your cousin—or your—

FINARD

She's no relation to me.

ROGER

Then she's your pupil?

FINARD

No more.

ROGER

I must still see her, know her—

FINARD

After the marriage won't you have plenty of time to get acquainted?

ROGER

Why, let me see the father—that's not too much, huh? I ask to see my father-in-law.

FINARD

I represent him.

ROGER

(aside) That's very flattering for him.

FINARD

And in seeing me—it's as if—

ROGER

But—but—

FINARD

Pardon, Chevalier, I must follow my instructions to the

letter. Your marriage will take place today—but only after winning your case. You see that we are frank and honest in business—After Court, we will conduct you to the Chapel where everything is prepared—I am going to prepare myself to have the honor of accompanying you myself.

(goes to left)

ROGER

But, yet once, more—my fiancée, sir, my fiancée?

FINARD

In a moment, I will present her to you.

(bowing)

ROGER

At last, I am going to see this mysterious creature. Ah! I shiver in advance! A father obliged to employ such means to place his daughter—evidently, she's some little monster that has been hidden from all eyes and who they rid themselves of in my favor—come—only filial devotion could make me decide on such a sacrifice.

(he sits down to the right, plunged in his reflections)

AFGHANO

(entering by the back and aside) I was sure of it—my adversary is here—established as if he were at home—while I—oh—the betrayal is flagrant.

ROGER

Who's coming there?

(rising and looking at Afghano) By Jove—this one is even uglier than the other one. This must be my father-in-law.

AFGHANO

(bowing) You are the Chevalier d'Anguilhem?

ROGER

Sir, I have no reason to hide my name—but I ask the same frankness of you—you are—

AFGHANO

An adversary—an enemy—

ROGER

Right—I prefer that. One knows right away with whom one is dealing—but what is the motive for the hostility with which you honor me?

AFGHANO

A trifle—an inheritance of 1,500 thousand pounds.

ROGER

Mr. Afghano.

AFGHANO

Himself.

ROGER

(aside) What hope!

(aloud) Ah, by Jove! My dear enemy—be welcome in this accursed house.

AFGHANO

Accursed house! Yet it seem that you've been given a grand welcome here.

ROGER

By people that cut throats or strangle you—

AFGHANO

What language.

(aside) Could he be less advanced than I thought?

ROGER

I repeat to you, I am enchanted to see you, and I hope we can understand each other.

AFGHANO

Understand each other?

ROGER

Without a doubt—if you are reasonable. To the devil with chicanery! No more battles, lawsuits between us! Let's arrange this in a friendly way and let's laugh at the black robes and square hats.

AFGHANO

What do you mean?

ROGER

I mean we must turn to our profit the morale of the fable—let us share the oil before the trial and throw the dregs to the judges.

AFGHANO

(aside) He wants to settle. My suspicions lacked common sense.

ROGER

You are considering my proposition—is it seducing—huh?

AFGHANO

It is inadmissible.

ROGER

Why?

AFGHANO

I am sure of winning.

ROGER

With the law is one ever sure of anything?

AFGHANO

My case is excellent.

ROGER

Mine is perhaps even better at this moment.

AFGHANO

Why then are you proposing a share to me?

ROGER

Oh! That's another matter—I have a hidden motive for that.

(aside) A villainous strong one!

(aloud) Heavens, sir, I am a fair player—I will leave your half of the inheritance.

AFGHANO

You are very generous, sir—

ROGER

You accept?

AFGHANO

I refuse.

(goes to sit at the table at the lift and sits himself to writing)

TOURANGEAU

(very agitated, entering from the back) My master, my dear master—at last I've found you!

ROGER

What do you want with me? What's wrong—look?

TOURANGEAU

(mysteriously) Ah—sir—!

ROGER

Well?

TOURANGEAU

Ah, sir—

ROGER

Will you come to the point?

TOURANGEAU

I think I've seen her.

ROGER

Who?

TOURANGEAU

She came, in by a little door—mysteriously—

ROGER

But who?

TOURANGEAU

A woman—when I say a woman—

ROGER

What woman?

TOURANGEAU

Yours!

ROGER

The Devil! Look—explain yourself—speak quickly—

(looking at Afghano) And be careful to speak low.

TOURANGEAU

(low) Imagine, sir, I was down there, under the vestibule, talking familiarity with the carriage horses that brought us here—horses that are not proud, although great lords—suddenly, I see a creature appear. Oh, but what a creature—

ROGER

What creature?

TOURANGEAU

A creature of the feminine sex—heavily veiled. But a blast of wind pushed aside the cloth—and I discovered, I saw.

ROGER

Well—?

TOURANGEAU

The most hideous thing a single eye—? And what an eye—and hair—and ferocious red hair—an old porter who was there assured me she had a silver arm—still, if it was hallmarked, it would make a vessel in a household—but I am sure it must be vile plate.

ROGER

Enough! Enough! Imbecile—you are giving me goose bumps.

TOURANGEAU

What would it have been, sir, if you had enjoyed the sight of her?

ROGER

Oh—I have to get out of this terrible snare at all costs.

AFGHANO

(aside, folding the letter he has just written) I cannot see the Councilor, but, but I will indeed find a way to get this letter to him before the hearing. My case is won!

ROGER

(reflecting) Yes—I've only this resource left—let's try again.

(going to Afghano) A word, sir—when you have finished your correspondence.

AFGHANO

(rising) I am listening to you, sir—what do you want?

ROGER

Just now to end all legal argument between us—I proposed to give you half the inheritance in litigation.

AFGHANO

And I refused, sir—

ROGER

Well—now, I will abandon two-thirds to you.

AFGHANO

(with irony) You despair of your cause so much?

ROGER

Why, to the contrary—look, sir—a million—cool million for you—without running any risk—there's an honest proposition—what the devil—?

AFGHANO

All or nothing, sir—that's my response.

ROGER

(as if struck by an idea) Well, yes, sir—the entirety—for you or for me—but without a trial—without the hangers on of the legal system.

AFGHANO

What do you mean?

ROGER

The whole thing—to the survivor—without discussion—without contest.

AFGHANO

I don't understand.

ROGER

Let's arrange things here—sword in hand—in a friendly way.

AFGHANO

A duel?

ROGER

A little duel to the death—a duel for 1,500 thousand pounds. Have people fought for reasons as good as these? Ah! I read in your eyes that this game agrees with you—it's the affair of a moment—come on, sir!

AFGHANO

For goodness sake!

ROGER

En garde!

TOURANGEAU

(coming forward to Roger) Sir!

ROGER

(to Tourangeau) Get back!

AFGHANO

Will you stop this!

ROGER

Oh—I won't release you! You will fight?

AFGHANO

I will not fight!

ROGER

It will be the judgment of God! By Jove—I prefer it to the judgment of men—let heaven pronounce between us— Come on—En garde!

AFGHANO

What a hothead!

ROGER

Must you be insulted to your face to put courage in your heart? You are a joker, a scoundrel—cheat—a wretch—

(he pulls him to him)

TOGETHER

(singing) Let's fight—fury will guide me!
Between us—let heaven decide
Without delay
Without trial
This way.
The two of us—
Sword in hand
Can reach an understanding.

AFGHANO

(singing) Help! Fury is guiding him—
Save me—his homicidal rage—
Will finish me off without delay—
Because I am going to win the trial today.

TOURANGEAU

(singing) Ah great God! Fury is guiding him—stop—his homicidal rage will end the trial—to be heard today—without any delay.

(Afghano leaves excitedly.)

ROGER

(putting his sword in his scabbard) The coward! The coward!

TOURANGEAU

Calm yourself, Chevalier, calm yourself—

ROGER

How can I calm down when I am going to marry—who? Who? An ignoble creature, a reject, a disgrace to nature!

TOURANGEAU

The fact is I've never seen a being so—phenomenal—and I've been to the circus.

(Eight persons—men and women—dressed severely enter one after the other, bow and silently assume places on all sides of the stage—Roger returns bow for bow.)

FINARD

(entering from the left) Chevalier d'Anguilhem—let your impatience be satisfied—I am going to present at last your finance to you—

ROGER

(aside) Good God!

TOURANGEAU

(aside) At last, we are going to see.

FINARD

(going to the door through which he came—) Come, come, Miss—

(Sylvandire enters with a very thick veil.)

TOURANGEAU

(aside) We are going to see that we shall see nothing at all.

FINARD

(leading Sylvandire by the hand) Your future spouse, the Chevalier, Roger Tancred d'Anguilhem.

(she makes a deep curtsy)

TOURANGEAU

(trying to get a look at her) Not a little hole, not a wedge.

ROGER

(without hesitation) Miss does not deign to remove the veil?

FINARD

Now—not at all, not at all—

ROGER

Still, it seems to me, sir—

FINARD

After the marriage, not before—

ROGER

(aside) He clings to that! No more doubt—she's something horrible.

FINARD

But, don't worry—you won't have long to wait—the trial is being decided at this moment—from the tribunal to the Chapel is just a step—the carriage is waiting for us—we can leave—

TOURANGEAU

(low to Roger) Don't go there, sir—don't go there—same figure, same—she's the one I saw, for certain.

ROGER

(aside) What to do? I promised, I signed—come—in

the hands of God!

(Finard gives his hand to Sylvandire—Roger follows; the guests give a hand to the ladies and leave. The music stops.)

TOURANGEAU

He's going there—he's walking—he's running—what a union. My God—ah, this revolts me—this exasperates me. To think I shall see such a handsome young man, my double coupled to such a deformity.

POUSETTE

(furtively opening the door at the right) Well, lad?

TOURANGEAU

Huh? What? What is it? Ah, it's you, Miss Pousette.

POUSETTE

(entering) Do I frighten you?

TOURANGEAU

You—frighten—oh, indeed—to the contrary—your sight more than ever diverts my masculine eye—but what did you come here to do?

POUSETTE

I left Afghano, who is going triumphantly to the hearing, and I am running with all haste, to warn the Chevalier to keep up his guard.

TOURANGEAU

Keep us his guard! Ah, my God! What must be done!

POUSETTE

Above all, he must escape the snares offered by the honest Finard—where is your master?

TOURANGEAU

Getting married.

POUSETTE

Already?

TOURANGEAU

For the last quarter hour.

POUSETTE

And the intended?

TOURANGEAU

Oh!

POUSETTE

You've seen her?

TOURANGEAU

Oh!

POUSETTE

Is she pretty?

TOURANGEAU

Oh!

POUSETTE

And your master knows her?

TOURANGEAU

No—since up till now she's veiled her charms—but as for me, I observed her—by a lucky stroke! What a head! What eyes!

(Enter d'Herbigny, de Villiers.)

D'HERBIGNY

Victory! Victory! Our friend has one his case.

DE VILLIERS

On all points.

D'HERBIGNY

He will be put in immediate possession of all the wealth of the late Vicomte de Bouzenois—movable and immovable.

DE VILLIERS

And the Lord Afghano, called the Indian, will pay the expenses without reserve or costs.

POUSETTE

And have you seen the Chevalier?

(Tourangeau goes back.)

D'HERBIGNY

No—when we arrived at the Palace, he had already left the Court.

POUSETTE

Poor Roger.

D'HERBIGNY

What do you mean, poor? Damn—I'd really like to be in his place—an inheritance of 1,500 thousand pounds—a magnificent hotel in Paris.

POUSETTE

But the wife, the wife—

D'HERBIGNY

Superfluous thing, that!

POUSETTE

It seems she's a miracle of ugliness—a phenomena of deformities.

TOURANGEAU

(at the door at back) Silence! Here are the newlyweds.

(Enter Roger, Sylvandire still veiled, and the guests.)

D'HERBIGNY, DE VILLIERS, POUSETTE, & TOURANGEAU

(singing) Here they are
And this poor husband
—Unlucky from the provinces
Is married
What a horror
To a phoenix of ugliness
Ah—let's pity his plight.

ROGER

(singing) It's all over.
My fate is accomplished
Unlucky
from the provinces.
I am going to see
what a horror
A real prodigy
of ugliness
Ah, what a misfortune for me.

FINARD and CHORUS

(singing) Here we are
But the poor husband
Unlucky
from the provinces
Far from believing in his luck
At the moment trembles in fear—

Ah—how great is his terror.

(Finard presents Sylvandire to parents and friends.)

ROGER

(with a very sad air) Hello, my friends, hello—

D'HERBIGNY

(sadly) Receive my congratulations, Chevalier.

ROGER

(in a low voice to d'Herbigny) Alas, my dear Vicomte, I believe I really gambled, and whoever wins—loses—

POUSETTE

(to Roger) Ah, indeed, is your wife always going to keep on her veil? A blindfold is good for love—but she—

ROGER

I tremble to unveil this frightful mystery.

POUSETTE

Come on—some courage! You must know what to reckon on—

(Sylvandire and Finard have taken seats.)

ROGER

(approaching Sylvandire, greatly embarrassed) Well, Miss—Madame—I mean—

SYLVANDIRE

Well, sir—

ROGER

(aside) Her voice is soft enough.

(aloud) Isn't it a really bizarre idea, really wild, that your father had? To marry us without permitting us to see each other?

SYLVANDIRE

My father had excellent reasons, without doubt, sir—but if the idea was wild—what name does the man who executed it deserve?

ROGER

(turning towards his friends) That wasn't a very bad answer.

POUSETTE

No, she's logical enough.

ROGER

(to Sylvandire) It was only through the most passive obedience that I could obtain your hand—charming—

SYLVANDIRE

And win your case—

ROGER

Madame.

SYLVANDIRE

Oh—never mind, sir—I hope you won't repent what you've done when you become acquainted with my character.

TOURANGEAU

(aside) Her character—but her nose!

SYLVANDIRE

I am not speaking of outward appearances—a philosopher counts them as nothing.

POUSETTE

Yi! Yi! Yi! Philosophy!

ROGER

(aside) We are there! I tremble!

SYLVANDIRE

Beauty is such a fragile benefit.

(singing) For a face they admire
A frivolous heart
A loose heart
I know—let's itself be seduced—
But alas,
Once that gift is gone,
one day or the other can change it—
Features ravishing, fresh and graceful
Time withers all in its course—
Like a flash—beauty passes.

ROGER

(singing to his friends) But ugliness is forever—

SYLVANDIRE

Aren't you of my opinion, Chevalier!

ROGER

Eh! Eh!

TOURANGEAU

Eh! Eh!

ROGER

(aside) She has some wit—

(aloud) But tell me, Madame—the motives which engage your father to hide you from all eyes—no longer exist?

TOURANGEAU

(aside) I should say so—now this trick is complete.

SYLVANDIRE

It's true, sir—

ROGER

Then this veil.

SYLVANDIRE

Will fall when you order it—aren't you my lord and master?

TOURANGEAU

(aside) Wheedler, go way!

ROGER

(aside) Ah—Great God—but look how I tremble—never mind—it's too late.

(aloud) Madame, would you, I conjure you—show us your features.

SYLVANDIRE

(removing her veil) You are obeyed, sir—

ROGER

(transported) What do I see—! O heaven—is it possible?

ALL

(singing) How gorgeous she is!
My heart is reborn at last
He's—
No more worries
How many charms—
Ah—what a happy marriage!

ROGER

How many attractions! This is a dream
That offers itself to one transported heart.

ALL

Great God
May he prolong it
To my enchanted eyes

ROGER

(in ecstasy) Ah! Madame! Excuse me—surprise—joy. I must ask your mercy for suspecting—

SYLVANDIRE

You are pardoned, sir—

(de Villiers and d'Herbigny approach Sylvandire, bow to her and exchange some words—while Roger and Pousette speak—then they pass to the right.)

ROGER

(aside—frightened) Ah, my God—but now I think of it—

POUSETTE

(in a low voice) What's wrong with you, Chevalier?

ROGER

Such a sweet person must already have been loved by someone, at least unless they kept her hidden in a closet.

POUSETTE

Is she as pretty as Constance?

ROGER

Doubtless—but I was sure of Constance.

POUSETTE

Ah, Chevalier, you are becoming shockingly demanding.

FINARD

Now, sir—allow us to put you in possession of your rich inheritance—we are going to return to the Hotel Bouzenois.

SYLVANDIRE

Where you will be received by my father.

FINARD

The Honorable Judge Bouteau, Councilor—Reporter

to the King in the High Chamber.

POUSETTE

Judge Bouteau.

D'HERBIGNY

The upright Judge!

DE VILLIERS

The incorruptible.

POUSETTE

Ah—everything is finally clear!

CHORUS

(singing) Let's leave—hurry let us take them to the brilliant hotel
Where all is seductive
Where joy awaits them.

ROGER

Let's go—what luck to take you to this brilliant hotel—
Where all is seductive
Where joy awaits us—

(Music.)

FINARD

Well, Chevalier—are you satisfied with your humble servant—has he fulfilled all the conditions properly?

ROGER

(low, looking at Sylvandire) There remains one final one, Mr. Finard—and tomorrow morning, if it is kept as faithfully as the others—there will be 100 crowns for you.

(aside) God! I think he made a face!

TOGETHER

(refrain) Let's hasten to take them—eh
May happiness lead you—eh
Hurry to take me—eh.

CURTAIN

ACT III

A reception room richly furnished in the Hotel Bouzenois, door at the back—side doors—two at the left one at the right—a table at the left with an elegant box at the left with an elegant box on it—armchairs—chairs—sofa to the right.

TOURANGEAU

(dressed as a valet de chamber at the door at the rear) Get to your posts, rogues! Listen for the bell—may the chambermaids hold themselves in readiness for the ladies of Madame.

(leaving the door) It's noon and the newlyweds haven't rung.

(listening at the door at the left) Nothing, nothing! The Chevalier is having a good sleep. After all, you will tell me—

(laughing) Eh, eh, eh—ah, I heard some noise—could my noble master have risen without the aid of his first Valet de Chamber? For I've been promoted to that dignity—why yes—God forgive me—here's my master.

ROGER

(enter in a richly brocaded robe—from the left) Ah, it's you, Tourangeau? Well—how did you spend the night, my lad?

TOURANGEAU

Me, sir? Me? Oh, my God, like usual with Christophe—he'd been really restless—he just stomped around all night—it's quite simple—he wanted to dance at your wedding, but say, sir—it's rather for me than for you to ask how you spend the night—for finally—

ROGER

(patting him on the cheek) Ah, wise guy—open that box—

(Roger sits on the sofa and points to the box.)

ROGER

The response is—open the box?

ROGER

Yes—that's the response.

TOURANGEAU

(to himself—opening the box) For goodness sake—I don't see the least connection.

ROGER

Take a purse which is there and bear it, yourself—on my behalf—to that honest and virtuous Mr. Finard—you know—

TOURANGEAU

Why, sir—he's been here since dawn. He's waiting for you to rise.

ROGER

Ah! He is here—then give me—

(Tourangeau gives him the purse from the box!)

ROGER

And have him come in—right now—this phoenix of lawyers!

TOURANGEAU

He didn't want to reply to my question. Between compatriots—one ought to do so—that's so.

(opens the door at the back) Enter, sir, enter—

(he leaves)

ROGER

(still seated) Come in then, Mr. Finard, come on in.

FINARD

(sly and bowing) The Chevalier will allow me?

ROGER

Here's my reply—honorable Mr. Finard.

(gives him a purse)

FINARD

(bowing humbly) No one is more gracious and more punctual.

ROGER

(rising and going to the box removing a second purse) That's not all—open your eyes and your ears. What's this?

FINARD

A second purse.

ROGER

And just like the first. And like the first it contains a hundred crowns.

FINARD

A hundred crowns!

ROGER

A hundred crowns. Well, this purse is destined to Mr. Gitomer on the condition he answers frankly my questions. Let him tell the truth, nothing but the truth. See—frankness—frankness for 100 crowns—they don't usually give you as much to lie—and it's more difficult it seems to me.

FINARD

Let the Chevalier question me and I am ready to respond.

ROGER

Well, now that these things are concluded, how is it that the excellent Judge Boutean, Councillor—reporter chose me in preference to all others to have me marry his daughter in such a bizarre manner—she's rich, wise, beautiful and must not lack brilliant opportunities at least with financiers and lawyers.

FINARD

Without offending your modesty, sir, I will reply first of all that a gentleman of your name and appearance can only flatter the hopes of a father-in-law—not mentioning an inheritance of 1,500 thousand pounds which is not met with every day.

ROGER

The dear judge knew the fortune of my Uncle de Bouzenois so perfectly?

FINARD

To the pound, penny and half penny! He had promised to endow his adorable daughter with the first fine case that came his way. Then he had a choice between you and your adversary—who parenthetically left his very night furious and swearing vengeance. But as you were a color more agreeable than his—he gave you preference.

ROGER

Let's return to Sylvandire—tell me this—between you and me—look—doesn't she have some defect in her character—some—

FINARD

Oh—she's perfection personified. Her godmother was

a fairy.

ROGER

But—isn't she a coquette?

FINARD

She was raised in a convent.

ROGER

Prodigal?

FINARD

She's the daughter of a procurer.

ROGER

Gambler?

FINARD

She's never touched a card.

ROGER

Gourmand?

FINARD

She lives in perfumes and roses, likes bees and butterflies—but sir—why these questions—mercy? You ought to have confidence in us—by now.

ROGER

None whatsoever, I confess it to you, my dear Mr. Finard; my answer is frank.

FINARD

And not very flattering—up till now have you been deceived by your humble servant?

ROGER

No—and perhaps I'm wrong to be so alarmed—but—

FINARD

Enjoy the present, sir—and have faith in the future and especially in your wife—she's a model of grace, candor and virtue—I swear to it to you—word of—

ROGER

(stopping him) No, no—no others—the devil! I much prefer to believe looking at Sylvandire—her features so candid and so pure—

FINARD

Yes, Chevalier, yes—I repeat to you—trust in your

wife—she's an angel—and it would be suspecting her still and slandering his even to withhold any longer this second purse from a loyal servant who has told you the complete truth.

ROGER

So be it, Mr. Finard.

(gives him the purse)

FINARD

Ah, what nobility, what generosity!

(bowing) Completely yours, Chevalier, completely yours!

ROGER

(turning his back on him) Your servant, Mr. Finard, your servant.

FINARD

(aside) Now, let's execute the orders of the Marquis de Royancourt.

(He bows and goes out by the back.)

ROGER

I don't know—but the face of that man inspires me with distrust and despite myself, I still believe in some trick—some machination—Sylvandire—so young, so beautiful—ah—this is really provincial—why—here I am going to be jealous if my wife—of a treasure they've given me, as they were saying—

(sings) She's a treasure, yes, I believe it—no doubt—
As charming to me as a princess—
So—up to now, knowing what it costs me—
I must also keep it as best I can.
For a treasure so dear—without being avaricious.
Prudent husband—fearing to be robbed.
It's indeed the least—for a treasure so rare
To have care of putting it under the key.
Yes, this treasure so rare so and so fragile.
I shall take care to keep locked up!

ROGER

(running to Sylvandire, who enters from the left) What! So early—my beautiful.

SYLVANDIRE

You were no longer there—I got bored.

ROGER

Then it was me you were looking for?

SYLVANDIRE

Certainly.

ROGER

Why you know you are adorable?

SYLVANDIRE

Tell me—what are you thinking?

ROGER

My word—yes—on honor of the present at least.

SYLVANDIRE

You already doubt the future?

ROGER

(leading her to the right) We know each other so little.

SYLVANDIRE

We will make ourselves acquainted.

(they sit on the sofa)

ROGER

I ask nothing better. And first of all, we ought to tell

each other frankly our plans for the future.

SYLVANDIRE

Our plans for the future?

ROGER

Yes—you indeed made some little plan in marrying me?

SYLVANDIRE

I formed the plan of loving you.

ROGER

There is nothing more loveable than that. But indeed you have some desire—

SYLVANDIRE

I have the desire of pleasing you.

ROGER

Better and better! But still—do you prefer Paris or the country?

SYLVANDIRE

Wherever you are, my friend, I will like.

ROGER

Then my darling friend, if you would like to please me.

SYLVANDIRE

Speak—

ROGER

You don't know my parents?

SYLVANDIRE

No—but I will be happy to know them.

ROGER

Well—that would happen by spending several days in Touraine.

SYLVANDIRE

Willingly.

ROGER

What—you'll consent?

SYLVANDIRE

With the greatest pleasure.

ROGER

My dear Sylvandire—you are an angel!

SYLVANDIRE

And when shall we leave?

ROGER

Whenever you wish, darling friend.

SYLVANDIRE

As soon as possible.

ROGER

Tomorrow.

SYLVANDIRE

So be it.

ROGER

Well, dear friend, I am going to give orders on my side—give orders on yours.

SYLVANDIRE

Tomorrow: We shall depart.

ROGER

(kissing her hand) What a delightful trip we're going to make.

(singing) Happy spouses—
Love accompanies us—
And pleasure smiles on the two of us.
Rest so sweet—that one finds in the country.
We'll please even better—
Our loving heart—

TOGETHER

Happy spouses, etc.

(Roger goes out by the left.)

(As soon as Roger leaves, Finette opens the door and speaks to Finard.)

FINETTE

You can come in, Mr. Finard, Madame is alone.

SYLVANDIRE

What's the matter?

FINETTE

Mr. Finard wants to speak to you, Madame.

(She leaves after Finard enters.)

SYLVANDIRE

(with urgency) Come in, Mr. Finard, come in—how is my father?

FINARD

Marvelous, Madame, marvelous. But the affairs of the Palace don't leave him a minute. He's overwhelmed.

SYLVANDIRE

Poor father!

FINARD

And he sent me to Madame to learn.

SYLVANDIRE

Oh—my good Finard—tell him I am very content, really happy.

FINARD

That will be a sweet balm for his paternal heart—for he only thinks of his dear child.

SYLVANDIRE

That good father! Raised far from him in a convent I hardly knew him—I even doubted him—and this marriage—how much it frightened me. Damn! To leave a cloister to marry like this—so suddenly it's terrifying. But I see now my father was right in telling me to let him do it—that he only wanted my happiness.

FINARD

Positively—

SYLVANDIRE

Also, I am touched by all his bounties—and by yours, too, Mr. Finard—and my gratitude.

FINARD

The best proof of that Madame can give us of it, is to continue to be docile and to follow all our advice blindly—

SYLVANDIRE

Isn't that my duty?

FINARD

Doubtless—moreover, Madame is very young—and leaving the cloister thrown into the hurley-burley of an entirely new world—she needs advice—excellent advice.

SYLVANDIRE

Oh—without doubt—but isn't my husband here? He has some experience—and he'll be really sweet to me.

FINARD

The Chevalier d'Anguilhem is a charming young man—but he comes form the depth of his province—he himself needs to be guided—carefully escorted. And Madame in the interest of his future.

SYLVANDIRE

Speak! What must he do—believe indeed.

FINARD

(pulling a letter from his pocket) My honorable patron, and I, his unworthy servant, we've drawn up some instructions—fruit of long usage—and which may be for Madame, a rule of conduct in regard to her noble spouse.

SYLVANDIRE

(taking the letter) Oh! Give me, Mr. Finard, give me—

FINARD

You understand that the Chevalier need not know.

SYLVANDIRE

Why's that?

FINARD

For a household to always be good, happy—the wife must assume an authority, an empire over her husband—but without his noticing it—without his even suspecting it. Advice is sweet to listen to and more easy to follow when it proceeds from a charming and adored mouth. You understand, Madame.

SYLVANDIRE

No—not completely—but I am going to read this paper instantly and I will do what you tell me—I promise you—for you've already proven that you are only seeking to make me happy.

FINARD

That's a task I've imposed on myself and which is very sweet to me—I will then tell my honored patron.

SYLVANDIRE

That all his advice and yours will be orders to me.

FINARD

(aside) Marvelous!

(aloud and bowing) Your very humble, Madame, accept, I beg you, the new assurance of my respect and my complete devotion—

(leaves by the back)

SYLVANDIRE

That excellent father—and when I think that in the convent I thought he didn't love me—oh, that made me really ill—how I was deceived—oh yes—I intend to follow his good advice—

(opening the letter) Lets see, let's see—

(reading with her eyes) Why yes—all this seems very wise to me—a powerful lord at the court has an interest in our family—he wants to protect my husband and me—he wants to obtain for Roger—oh—why that will be charming—they fear my husband might refuse—

Oh—no—as the excellent Mr. Finard said—I must surely have some empire over his heart—and I hope indeed to decide him—It goes to his future and the luster of his name—! And I intend to be proud of my husband!

ROGER

(coming in the left) All the orders are given and tomorrow after lunch we will leave—well, what's the matter, dear friend?

SYLVANDIRE

I am looking at you.

ROGER

You're looking at me?

SYLVANDIRE

Do you know, sir, you have a fine appearance.

ROGER

Oh—when I've spent three or four years in Paris, I won't be more ridiculous than anyone else.

SYLVANDIRE

How fine you would look in a colonel's uniform.

ROGER

Me?

SYLVANDIRE

Yes—you haven't you ever thought of having a regiment?

ROGER

Indeed, Sylvandire—but it's not an easy thing, dear Sylvandire—plague! A regiment—how you do go on!

SYLVANDIRE

Well! Would you like for me to give you one?

ROGER

(laughing) You? And how would you do that? Allow me to tell you, my dear, Sylvandire that you have charming dreams—but they are only dreams unfortunately.

SYLVANDIRE

Which we will make into realities when you wish.

ROGER

Are you ambitious, Sylvandire?

SYLVANDIRE

Oh—only for you—I would like to see you at Court—

haven't you ever thought of going to Court?

ROGER

Indeed—but as for me, a provincial gentleman—what do you expect?

SYLVANDIRE

Aren't you from one of the first families of Touraine?

ROGER

Yes.

SYLVANDIRE

Don't you have sixty thousand pounds income?

ROGER

Yes—

SYLVANDIRE

Don't you have one of the most magnificent hotels in Paris?

ROGER

Yes—

SYLVANDIRE

Ah, I understand—you would be ashamed of me—

ROGER

Of you, darling Sylvandire?

SYLVANDIRE

(lowing her eyes) You fear my naivety?

ROGER

You're as witty as a demon.

SYLVANDIRE

My clumsiness?

ROGER

You are graceful as a sylph.

SYLVANDIRE

My ugliness?

ROGER

You are beautiful as a star—

SYLVANDIRE

Well, my friend, since you are young, brave and rich—and you are so kind as not to find me too bad—why go so quickly to the provinces, why not appear at Court?

ROGER

My word—you might indeed be right.

SYLVANDIRE

Your parents love you, I don't doubt it, they desire to see you, I am really certain of it—but don't you think they will pardon you this slight delay when you come to them with a Colonel's epaulets and a wife presented at Court?

ROGER

That is to say they would be enchanted.

SYLVANDIRE

You see—you see—well, you must occupy yourself with this today even—

ROGER

What must I do?

SYLVANDIRE

Not a thing! Didn't I tell you this was my business?

ROGER

(laughing) But really dear friend—I can't imagine—you wouldn't be a fairy?

SYLVANDIRE

Perhaps a good fairy for you. Let's go, sir—let yourself be led by the ring—

(to Finette who enters) What do you want, Finette?

FINETTE

I ask pardon of Madame for coming this way—if it weren't for a good action, I wouldn't allow myself.

ROGER

For a good action, dear Sylvandire.

FINETTE

It's a lady of charity who collects for the orphans.

SYLVANDIRE

Ah—you did well, Finette—and where is this lady of

charity?

FINETTE

I had her go into your room, Madame.

(she goes out by the left)

SYLVANDIRE

Would you excuse me, my friend?

ROGER

How can you ask!

SYLVANDIRE

(singing) Forgive me if I leave you. When misfortune invites me, they never in vain
Never in vain
Invoke my charity for the neighbor.

ROGER

(singing) In you, my all beautiful are joined all the virtues.
Each instant reveals to me—
An additional charm.

TOGETHER

(singing) With regret I leave you.
But return very quickly
—They never in vain
Invoke your interest
For the neighbor.

SYLVANDIRE

(singing) Forgive me if I leave you, etc.

(she goes out to he left.)

ROGER

(alone) Ah, indeed—why this is a perfect wife I've got there—despite his foxy mug, Finard spoke the truth—one wishes, indeed, to making something like this that it would not come to an end—!

(Enter lackey, announcing.)

LACKEY

The Count d'Herbigny—Mr. de Villiers.

(Enter d'Herbigny and de Villiers.)

ROGER

Ah, gentlemen—be welcome.

D'HERBIGNY

The manner in which you receive as indicates to us that we must congratulate you—therefore receive our congratulations.

ROGER

I receive them; since yesterday I've gone from one surprise to the next and each more agreeable than the last.

DE VILLIERS

So much the better! Let's pray God it will last—aren't you going to present us to Madame d'Anguilhem?

ROGER

She's occupied at the moment, I think—but return to dine, without manners—as friends.

D'HERBIGNY

As friends?

ROGER

By Jove! Aren't you my friends?

D'HERBIGNY

Yes, but that's not a reason for us to be friends with Mr. d'Anguilhem. If the friends of the husband were always those of the wife—

DE VILLIERS

Those of the husband are rarely those of the wife.

D'HERBIGNY

But on the subject of friends, we were forgetting the principal purpose of our visit—a young and pretty person is waiting below in my carriage for permission to be presented to you—

ROGER

A young and pretty person—why make her wait?

TOURANGEAU

(entering at the rear, embarrassed) Sir—

ROGER

Well, what?

TOURANGEAU

It's that, seeing your real position as a newlywed—I

really don't know for sure—

ROGER

Look, get to the point, imbecile!

TOURANGEAU

I really don't know if I can bring myself to announce the person who is presenting herself.

ROGER

Why's that?

TOURANGEAU

It's not that she's not agreeable in every way, but—

D'HERBIGNY

(laughing) It's she!

ROGER

Who is it then?

D'HERBIGNY

What! You can't make it out? Eh—come on in.

TOURANGEAU

(announcing) Miss.

POUSETTE

(entering from the back) That's good—get out! I will announce myself indeed—your best friend, Roger—that's the name I want them to introduce me with to you.

ROGER

And you will always be welcome charming Pousette.

POUSETTE

I am coming here with reasons.

(low to d'Herbigny) Vicomte—leave me alone with Roger—I need to speak to him.

D'HERBIGNY

The devil! A tête-à-tête the day after his marriage. That's dangerous! At least with the regulation week—scalawag.

POUSETTE

Ah—don't joke.

D'HERBIGNY

Go on—remain together—my turtle dove.

POUSETTE

Still—don't go off too far. It may be Roger will have need of you.

D'HERBIGNY

Well! Where do you want me to wait for you?

ROGER

In my library.

POUSETTE

I won't be long in rejoining you.

DE VILLIERS

Chevalier—we are leaving you.

D'HERBIGNY

For the moment, of course—for we accept your dinner—

ROGER

Marvelous, gentlemen, and I beg you to consider my

table as your town.

TOGETHER

(singing) When friendship invites you—
Really, it's whole hearted
Ah, return quickly—
To share my luck—

D'HERBIGNY & DE VILLIERS

(singing) When friendship invites us—
Let's accept with all our heart
And we will quickly return
To share his luck—

D'HERBIGNY

Tell we meet again, very dear friend—and a continuation of surprises—

ROGER

No, now—word of honor, I prefer that all this stop here.

ALL TOGETHER

(refrain) When friendship invests us, etc.

(d'Herbigny and de Villiers go through the door at the right.)

ROGER

Well—dear friend—here we are alone—what have you to tell me—I saw you separate d'Herbigny and de Villiers and I presume—

POUSETTE

You presume—? Plague! What perspicacity.

ROGER

My dear, you don't know what a sharp eye I have since I've married—

POUSETTE

So much the better—that can be useful to you.

ROGER

Huh? What are you saying there?

POUSETTE

I am saying, my dear Chevalier, that marriage is an abnormal condition and it requires great philosophy.

ROGER

Pousette, my good friend, put yourself au courant right away—I've got a strong constitution and I don't need circumspection.

POUSETTE

Well! My poor Roger—you must know I've gotten my information on the house of Bouteau, Finard, and company—I have my police—your wife—

ROGER

They told you about her, too—? What could they have told you? You've seen her—she's pretty.

POUSETTE

Very pretty.

ROGER

She is witty.

POUSETTE

I know it.

ROGER

She's wise.

POUSETTE

Marvelously! But her wisdom hasn't prevented her

from being noticed by a powerful lord.

ROGER

Ah! The Devil! But her wisdom must doubtless have prevented her from noticing him.

POUSETTE

They say so—what is certain is that this handsome Marquis adores the daughter of Judge Bouteau—that for her—every Sunday he went to Mass—in the Chapel of the convent—to ogle the pretty pensionary.

ROGER

Every Sunday.

POUSETTE

Oh—he's a very religious man—what do I know—in giving the water of benediction a little letter is soon slipped—

ROGER

Pousette, my goddess—you will tell me the name of this man, won't you?

POUSETTE

He's the Marquis de Royancourt.

ROGER

De Royancourt—one of the best friends of Madame DuBarry!

POUSETTE

All powerful through her—disposing of regiments and letters de cachet neither more nor less than Mr de la Villiers! All the same, a charming cavalier.

ROGER

Then why didn't he marry Sylvandire?

POUSETTE

Listen—one doesn't do like that without being a little pressured—Marquise—daughter of a little lawyer. They find it more convenient in these times to wait until she's been provided a husband and give this husband a command in the provinces—or indeed a regiment.

ROGER

Pousette, my dear Pousette—you are on the track—word of honor—

POUSETTE

How's that?

ROGER

They've spoken to me about a regiment.

POUSETTE

Already!

ROGER

This morning.

POUSETTE

It would have been more delicate to mention it to you yesterday, damnation, my dear—these little ladies of the judiciary—they go like the devil!

ROGER

Yes—but we will go as fast as she.

POUSETTE

That's not so certain.

ROGER

What do you mean?

POUSETTE

It's not certain we will catch her.

ROGER

Why's that?

POUSETTE

Because she's got a head start on us.

ROGER

A head start on us?

POUSETTE

Sylvandire received a visit this morning.

ROGER

Yes, from a lady of charity.

POUSETTE

Very charitable indeed.

ROGER

Huh?

POUSETTE

I know her—she's the little messenger from the Opera—and the private messenger of the Marquis de Royancourt.

ROGER

And what did she come here for?

POUSETTE

Her job. Bring a letter.

ROGER

A letter from whom?

POUSETTE

A letter from the Marquis.

ROGER

You are sure, Pousette.

POUSETTE

Damn!

ROGER

My dear Pousette—every letter deserves a reply—

POUSETTE

That's my opinion.

ROGER

And Marquis de Royancourt shall have no reason to complain—for he will have two—

POUSETTE

Which is abundant doesn't corrupt.

ROGER

(going to the table at the left and preparing to write) My dear Pousette—treat me as stupid and caddish say my name is not Roger Tancred d'Anguilhem if—before the end of the next week there's not one Marquis less to make a pretty leg and an eye.

(writing) "Dear Marquis,

No bravado—he'll take me for a Gascon—no insults—he'll take me for someone from Limousin—!

(writing) It will take a week to accomplish a little trip I am going to make with Madame d'Anguilhem. I hope to have the pleasure of meeting you in the eighth day, in the Queen's Court at seven in the morning; I will be there with my sword and like a good gentleman who doesn't leave, without his—I hope to see you there with yours.

Chevalier d'Anguilhem."

POUSETTE

Bravo, my darling—now there's a challenge gallantly packaged—one would think you did nothing else in your life.

ROGER

My dear Pousette, take this letter to d'Herbigny and Villiers.

POUSETTE

I understand you—the Hotel de Royancourt is only two steps from here and in a quarter of an hour.

ROGER

Pousette, you are a charming woman—

POUSETTE

No? Pousette is a Mad Woman, a scatterbrain, who is really afraid of having advised you to do something stupid—do you understand? But Pousette is a sharp girl—clever and devoted—who will always be ready to render you a service. She has your honor at heart, you see and she won't suffer anyone to decorate with impunity your face with a co—

ROGER

Ahem!

POUSETTE

(with dignity) A colonel's hat—I didn't intend to say anything else Chevalier—I've got too much "couth" for that. Without goodbyes—till later, my darling.

(she goes out by the right)

ROGER

(alone) Ah, because I'm a good son, because I had to marry blindly to save my parents from misery they wanted to treat me like Georges Dandin—stop there, my little Marquis.

(singing) I'm not one of those vulgar husbands purchasing favor with shame.
One of those husbands who, like debonair sheep
In the Stag Park—put up with dishonor
My handsome Marquis—, that woods,
Whose origin was grafted badly in our noble forests
For the source perishes forever—
As for me, I'll cut it at its root.

(rings)

TOURANGEAU

(entering) Sir.

ROGER

Go hitch up the carriage and saddle Christophe.

TOURANGEAU

Saddle Christophe—disturb him—poor animal! What for?

ROGER

Why so Tourangeau can follow us to Anguilhem where we will spend a few days.

TOURANGEAU

(joyfully) What, sir, we are returning to Anguilhem! What! I am going to see my loves again! What! Christophe is going to return to the stable of his birth! In an instant all will be ready, sir, in an instant.

(goes out)

ROGER

(alone) It's the best thing to return to Anguilhem—Sylvandire will never see Paris again—and as for myself—I shall not reappear except to give this

Marquis a lesson—

SYLVANDIRE

(running in from the left) Roger! Roger! My friend!

(joyfully) How happy I am—

ROGER

What's the matter with you, Madame?

SYLVANDIRE

The commission as colonel—you will have it—this very day—they just let me know it this instant—oh, my friend, how happy I am!

ROGER

(with irony) And I owe this favor to—

SYLVANDIRE

A friend of my family—a protector who means you very well—

ROGER

Means me very well—yes—and he's keeping me from proving to him all my gratitude.

SYLVANDIRE

(astonished) But what's the matter with you, my friend? That air—that tone—you seem angry—when I thought you were going to thank me.

ROGER

(bitterly) I indeed owe you great thanks, Madame.

SYLVANDIRE

But mercy—answer—what's the matter with you?

ROGER

The matter, Madame, is—that I don't need your protector and that his protection costs too much.

SYLVANDIRE

What do you mean? I don't understand.

ROGER

(with rage) Ah, you don't understand? Well, I will make you understand—much later—but for the moment get ready to leave.

SYLVANDIRE

To leave?

ROGER

Yes, Madame—you are going to leave Paris—and forever.

SYLVANDIRE

Forever!

ROGER

Yes—the air is—unhealthy—especially for newly-weds.

SYLVANDIRE

You frighten me, Roger.

ROGER

It rains perfumed letters, and colonel's commissions—it's unhealthy!

SYLVANDIRE

My God! My God! What does all this mean?

ROGER

Come, Madame, come—you must submit—you must leave.

TOURANGEAU

(entering) Sir, here's a gentleman in black who asks to speak to you immediately.

ROGER

(impatiently) Let him come back in a week. I am not visible.

TOURANGEAU

That's what I told him, but he pretends to he comes in the name of the King.

ROGER

(surprised) In the name of the King!

TOURANGEAU

Indeed—as he has a black suit and a silver chain, I thought he might be attached to the court.

ROGER

Show him in.

(Tourangeau introduces the officer and leaves.)

(Music until the end of the act.)

OFFICER

You are indeed the Chevalier Roger Tancred d'Anguilhem?

ROGER

Yes, sir.

OFFICER

Chevalier, here is a double response to a very honest letter you wrote just now.

ROGER

(taking it and breaking the seal) A single word would suffice, sir—but I see with pleasure that he was diligent.

(perusing the papers) A Colonel's commission.

(glancing at the other) An order to place me in the Bastille! That's fine—for the day after the wedding—not slow.

OFFICER

It's your choice, Chevalier.

SYLVANDIRE

What's he say?

ROGER

In consideration of the former services of my father, sir, I could look at this commission as honorable, as a debt which His Majesty remembered—but today—it's an insult to me and that I reject.

(tears up the commission)

OFFICER

What—! You prefer—!

ROGER

The Bastille!

SYLVANDIRE

(despairing) The Bastille!

Why no—it's impossible.

(to the officer) Sir, sir—I entreat you.

(to Roger) My friend! In the name of heaven!

ROGER

(ironically) Marvelous, Madame—your surprise is very well acted.

OFFICER

(to Roger) Would you then, sir—

SYLVANDIRE

I won't leave you—! Sir, let me, let me follow you!

ROGER

(bitterly) Cease, cease, this unworthy comedy, Madame—and as for this Marquisk, tell him carefully that the decision is taken—and that we will find each other again.

ROGER

(to the Officer) Let's go, sir, I follow you.

SYLVANDIRE

What's he say? Roger! Roger!

ROGER

(pushing her away) Enough, enough—Madame—

(The Officer leaves, Roger remains at the back looking at Sylvandire until the curtain falls.)

SYLVANDIRE

Lord! Have pity on me.

(She collapses in a faint in an armchair on the left.)

CURTAIN

ACT IV

Aboard the tartene, the Zorah, *the captain's cabin—richly decorated in the asiatic fashion—two side doors—a back door with a grill through which one can see the ocean. Several cushions on the left.*

FINARD

(wrapped in a huge cape cap pulled down over his eyes) (mysteriously) So it's understood.

MULEI

Perfectly agreed—the Chevalier d'Anguilhem has a rendezvous here—aboard my vessel—

FINARD

With the Marquis de Royancourt—who will be an hour late—

MULEI

And during that hour—

FINARD

Hush!

(pause) Then I can tell the noble lord who honors me with his confidence.

MULEI

That all his wishes will be fulfilled.

FINARD

But the Marquis intends to be very certain that the Chevalier D'Anguilhem—

MULEI

That's fair! Return in an hour and you will see for yourself—

FINARD

(terrified) Me! If the Chevalier were to recognize me! The devil.

MULEI

In the midst of the tumult of the feast I am giving tonight on board my tartene you won't be recognized. Anyway one of my men will inform me of your arrival and you will have nothing to fear.

FINARD

Very good—we will say in an hour and I will deliver to you the sum promised.

MULEI

Thus we will be sure of one another.

FINARD

You know that this isn't all—if the Marquis is satisfied with you—in his capacity of Intendant of the Province—he will shut his eyes and let you make some little expeditions on the coast—from time to time—without troubles without bickering, you understand?

MULEI

Many thanks—in an hour then.

FINARD

In an hour—discretion—prudence!

MULEI

That belongs to my condition.

(Finard disappears to the right wrapped in his cloak.)

MULEI

Go, go—honest Christian—I shall no longer need the protection of Your Marquis. Allah protects me.

(sitting on the cushions at the left) And thanks to a certain business, I shall never have completed a more fruitful voyage than this one—yes, I shall have wherewithal to buy a pachalik. Come, that doesn't sound too bad—

(a sailor enters from the right) Well, what's the matter?

SAILOR

Captain, a sloop is coming to bring that pretty dancing girl from the Opera that's playing in Marseille, who you invited to come visit your tartene.

MULEI

Show her in, and bring tobacco and pipes.

(Pousette is shown in.)

MULEI

Be welcome, my beautiful houri—I was hoping you'd come, but I didn't expect you.

POUSETTE

(looking around her) Plague! It seems the profession of Corsair is very good and your cabin is almost as elegant.

MULEI

As the boudoir of a dancer, right, my beautiful Pousette. That's because both have a certain resemblance—they conquer the infidels.

POUSETTE

My, my, my for a Turk you are not lacking in a certain observation from what you are saying to me—ah, but indeed, it seems to me you really could get up, my friend, the Turk.

MULEI

On the contrary it's you who are going to sit down my beautiful Frenchie—

(The sailor has brought in a very low table on which is a platter with cups, coffee, sugar—he pushes two cushions near the table. Pousette sits. The sailor presents a pipe to Mulei and another to Pousette.)

POUSETTE

What's this?

MULEI

A chibouk of real latakia and a cup of pure mocha—

POUSETTE

(sitting) Go for your latakia and mocha—

(smoking) As for me, I was born to be a Sultana.

MULEI

There's no time to lose.

POUSETTE

Ah, indeed, say this, on the topic of sultanas—do you know I must have no end of courage—to come to your place like this.

MULEI

Courage! To be present at the feast I am giving this evening to the most refined women of Marseille—is that so frightening?

POUSETTE

Listen! It's because singular rumors are running on your account—Musselman?

MULEI

And what are they?

POUSETTE

They suspect you of trading in whites—

MULEI

What do you want?—they complained my lost shipment of blacks had a bad complexion.

POUSETTE

Then it's true then—that?

MULEI

By Allah! With all others, I wouldn't admit it, but with you, my dancing doll—

POUSETTE

Hey! Wait a minute—handsome brown fellow—don't go carrying me off into Barbary—as for me, I have nothing to do in that country. I have little inclination to harems, where you can only talk to mutes and other very disagreeable individuals.

MULEI

Don't worry—I am a conscientious merchant—ordinarily, I don't take, I purchase—

POUSETTE

And from whom do you purchase?

MULEI

Oh—from all hands—so long as my merchandise be fresh and pretty—

(singing) I'm not fussy—
Over the choice of my vendors—
But a clever negotiator
I know how to pay for the best—

POUSETTE

(laughing) (singing) The best—

MULEI

(singing) It's a chance which comes with this wind for I am stocking myself up in France.

POUSETTE

They must often rob you.

MULEI

Frankly—that happens to me sometimes—but with our Pashas from Smyrna and Trebizond. After that, I am rarely deceived—here, today I am just making a bizarre enough business and very advantageous.

POUSETTE

You've bought someone?

MULEI

On the contrary—they are paying me to rid them of someone—

POUSETTE

Ah! Ah!

MULEI

A great bargain—do you know a certain Marquis de Royancourt?

POUSETTE

Right! Could you have purchased, bad merchandise from him?

MULEI

Not at all—on the contrary, it's he who—

POUSETTE

(curious) Look, speak—what traffic have you had with him—

MULEI

Oh, none, none, but I must confess, he's a man very honest in business.

POUSETTE

(aside) The implacable enemy of Anguilhem relations with this miscreant—if the good Roger were in Marseille, I would tremble for him.

(aloud and gaily) So nice, my dear Turk—that you are satisfied—the speculation given on the Marseille side—

MULEI

But I am not complaining on that side.

POUSETTE

On what side are you complaining then?

MULEI

I complain on yours, I complain over your severity, I complain of having already thrown away five kerchiefs on you uselessly—what are you waiting for—beautiful Pousette?

POUSETTE

Heavens! I'm waiting for the sixth—so I will have a half-dozen.

TOURANGEAU

(entering from the right) Pardon, Mr. Turk, but it's I—

MULEI

Who are you?

TOURANGEAU

I, Tourangeau—

(noticing Pousette) Heavens! It's you, Miss Pousette—oh—how happy I am to see you again! By chance, were you made Turk, since you smoke like a Swiss and you drink like a Polish girl?

(Mulei pushes him away.)

POUSETTE

Ah, my God—but I am not mistaken—it really is him! It's Tourangeau! Look at me, imbecile!

TOURANGEAU

(going closer) Ah, you recognized me—surely, it's I—at least, unless they changed me at the customs depot!

MULEI

You know this lad, beautiful Pousette?

POUSETTE

(rising) Yes, Captain—he's even one of my admirers.

TOURANGEAU

Oh—yes—one of your admirers such that you can still boast of it.

MULEI

In that case I pardon him in your favor—

TOURANGEAU

What do you mean! You pardon me. What did I do?

MULEI

You entered without my permission!

TOURANGEAU

There's no one in the antechamber—besides, I came to announce to you that my noble Master, the Chevalier d'Anguilhem is going to accept the gallant invitation you gave him to visit your ship.

POUSETTE

What! The Chevalier is also in Marseille?

TOURANGEAU

Arrived day before yesterday—with your servant.

POUSETTE

(aside) Oh—oh decidedly there's something behind this—I really did well to come here.

MULEI

You are, you say, the slave of the young Chevalier d'Anguilhem?

TOURANGEAU

Gracious Musselman—I will make you the observation there are no slaves in France—we are all free—as they say—as for me, I am a household servant! But aside from that, I am my own master.

MULEI

And tell me, lad, what sort of man is the Chevalier?

TOURANGEAU

Why, the most beautiful sort, I beg you to believe a superb cavalier, full of wit, courage—and noble like the King.

MULEI

How old is he?

TOURANGEAU

Twenty-five years old, august Osmanli.

MULEI

Talents for—?

TOURANGEAU

Why he is full of accomplishments.

POUSETTE

(aside) What do all these questions signify? Is it by chance—ah, I will find out—

MULEI

And he's married, they tell me?

TOURANGEAU

That is to say, he was married to a charming woman—but they've been separated—seeing he was incarcerated in the Bastille—for eight months—he's got out, thanks to the efforts of his friend, the Vicomte d'Herbigny—a brave ship's captain.

MULEI

And then, he found his wife again?

TOURANGEAU

Not at all—he refused to see her again—why—he never wanted to tell me—he's a good master—but he's a bit secretive with me.

MULEI

That's fine—! In your turn now, dog of a Christian.

TOURANGEAU

What are you saying—dog of a Christian?—why that's very rude, that is.

MULEI

Oh, pay no attention—it's a Musselman expression. We Mahommetans call everybody dog—who's not a Turk.

TOURANGEAU

Heavens! With us it's just the reverse—we call Turk everything that's doglike—but you said—in my turn—what in my turn?

MULEI

Yes, in your turn—what do you know how to do? Are you capable of being Bostangi-Bachi?

TOURANGEAU

What's that you're saying? Boston what?

MULEI

Bostangi-Bachi—that is to say, gardener—you know digging, grafting, watering.

TOURANGEAU

Ah, indeed that's good! Why that's my primary job—being gardener—before being elevated to the grade of household servant, I was a peasant—but why do you ask me that, Lord?

MULEI

What a shrimp!

TOURANGEAU

Shrimp, I—why I say I really love them—I'm crazy about them in salads.

MULEI

(laughing) Come, come, I see that you are a good lad and we will understand each other marvelously.

SAILOR

(entering) The Chevalier d'Anguilhem has just come aboard.

MULEI

Ah! Very good—you will excuse me, beautiful Pousette—business above all.

POUSETTE

(surprising) For goodness sake—but I don't want you to abandon me so quickly—I only came here for you.

MULEI

I am going to escort you to my arsenal—my boudoir—where they will serve you a sorbet.

POUSETTE

I accept, handsome Almanzor—but above all, you must give me a bit of information that I need—you aren't going to be discreet with me.

MULEI

I will tell you what you want—on the condition you be less savage.

POUSETTE

Savage! Me! You have to be a Turk to believe that—

(low to Tourangeau) Not a word of me, do you hear, to whoever it may be—

TOURANGEAU

Suffice! Motus!

MULEI

(to Tourangeau) Beg your master to be so good as to wait for me a moment—

TOURANGEAU

I shan't fail, august Omar—(Pousette and Mulei go out left)

Well, this miscreant is not too disagreeable—only why did he ask me if I know how to water, to dig, what the devil can it be to him? Ah—Chevalier—

ROGER

(entering from the right) Nobody?

TOURANGEAU

Yes, indeed, sir, me first of all and then the Captain's going to come—they say the little party he's preparing aboard will be very diverting—

ROGER

(impatiently) Eh! What does his party matter to me? I am only coming here to have an affair with this Marquis de Royancourt—who's finally given me a rendezvous. He hasn't arrived yet.

TOURANGEAU

I don't know.

ROGER

So quickly then, and inform yourself if he's already here—stay on the bridge—watch for his arrival and the moment he appears, run warn me.

TOURANGEAU

Yes, sir—and while waiting for him I will talk a little with the Turkish sailors. I don't scorn the Turks—on the contrary they spend almost all their lives with their legs crossed—and they have swarms of women—I share these Musselman ideas.

ROGER

Go on! Go on!

TOURANGEAU

As you wish, sir—

(he goes out by the back)

ROGER

Ah! Let him come, this Marquis! Let him come—at last he accepts my challenge—he accepted it even more gallantly then I should have thought, but never mind—I will be pitiless towards him and I will kill the infamous fellow. As for his accomplice—as for her—who took my name to sully it—a cloister will do me justice. Ah, that woman—when I saw her for the first time—so beautiful—seeming so sweet—and so candid—what would have told me—and I felt so honestly disposed to love her—life was offering itself to me so frankly and so happily—young, rich—bearing a name which permitted me to aspire to anything! Ah, Marquis, Marquis! It's you who I'll pay for all that. You first of all, then she—at last I have them both.

POUSETTE

(entering from the left) Not yet, my darling.

ROGER

Pousette, here! How's that come about?

POUSETTE

You shall know, ingrate! If you had concerned yourself a little about me—you would have learned I'm playing in the great theater.

ROGER

But aboard this vessel—explain to me.

POUSETTE

By God—the explanation won't take long—Captain Omar saw me dance the part of a Zephyr in the ballet Venus and Adonis—where without boasting, I had a famous success—he sent me kerchief after kerchief—and finally got me to promise to come aboard his tartene today.

ROGER

And as you are a woman of your word you've been exact as to the rendezvous.

POUSETTE

Yes, I am exact luckily—not for the Moroccan whom I am simply mocking—for you, my gentleman.

ROGER

For me? For me? What do you mean, Pousette?

POUSETTE

I mean that during your eight months in the Bastille you ought to have thought of becoming prudent and political—the Royancourt knows where you are.

ROGER

Doubtless since I sent him a challenge.

POUSETTE

Marvelous—now there's prudence, a challenge to the Intendant of the Province.

ROGER

Eh—what's it matter—I repeat to you that I've got him, that he will fight and that I will kill the infamous fellow!

POUSETTE

If the infamous fellow gives you leisure—which you will permit me to doubt, my Cid—

ROGER

Here's his letter.

POUSETTE

(reading) "One can't refuse such a gracious invitation from someone who runs 200 leagues just to make it. The Captain of the *Zorah* is in the roadstead of Marseille—he's giving a party aboard. Under pretext of being present—rendezvous tomorrow on his ship—one of his sloops will take us to Pommergues—two of his officers will serve as witnesses—they will be unaware of the reason we are fighting—all this will take place in the most noble and secret way in the world—completely yours.

ROGER

You see it is difficult to be more clear.

POUSETTE

Yes, and yet you haven't seen a thing.

ROGER

I've seen he must come here and that I must wait for him.

POUSETTE

Well, while waiting you will soon voyage to the coasts of Barbary—does that please you?

ROGER

The Devil take me—I don't understand—

POUSETTE

Indeed, it's hard indeed to understand such a direct joke. In short, the dear Marquis, in concert with your charming spouse, who's coming without doubt to rejoin him—imagined the best way to rid himself of you once and for all was to make you travel with Captain Omar—who sails this very day for Tunis.

ROGER

Me! Me! Come on, what stupid story are you telling me?

POUSETTE

You will complete the cargo; you will leave tonight.

ROGER

No—no—it's impossible.

TOURANGEAU

(running in from the right, pale and trembling) Let's escape—let's escape—ah, Chevalier—ah, Miss Pousette!

ROGER

Well! What's happened?

TOURANGEAU

Let's escape, my master—let's all escape. Ah, indeed, yes—save ourselves—what am I saying—the Pirate has got us—he won't let us escape, the corsair.

ROGER

But what is it? Look—

TOURANGEAU

What is it? Didn't I tell you? We are lost. We've been sold.

ROGER

Sold—

TOURANGEAU

That horrible Omar—he ought to blush for it! Going to sell us—you and me—a little Moroccan that I know in Paris in the service of a Duchess and who's returning with his black comrades on this vessel, told me the thing—and asked me if I had accomplishments, the buccaneer—if I knew how to water a garden, the swine—you, too, Chevalier—he finds you to be a handsome man—that's sort of a consolation—they value you very highly—10,000 boudjous—but me, sir, but me, Miss—they are taking me below market. They charge two rupees for me—is that humiliating to be valued like that?

POUSETTE

Well, Chevalier, do you still doubt?

ROGER

What! It must be true! Oh—that infernal trap! O double traitor—yes, I recognize your work—praise God—

eight months in the Bastille was already much—but Tunis or Morocco—that shall not be, death of my life.

(furious) Sword out! Damn! And let them give me free passage. They'd better stay out of my way.

(half drawing his sword)

POUSETTE

(calmly stopping him) Patience—gunpowder—and hear me—I told you that Captain Omar does what I want—

ROGER

Well—

POUSETTE

Its he who told me these agreeable plans that your friend, the Marquis has for you. It's he who after having bought you consented to resell you.

ROGER

To resell me?

POUSETTE

Yes, to me—it's I who repurchased you—at a very dear price but I am really counting on not paying it—

to a corsair, a dancer, and a courtesan. We will see who will win—meanwhile you belong to me—

ROGER

Still, I cannot—

POUSETTE

You can do all I wish—I am going to find my friend the Turk again—he will secretly escort you to land in a pretty little sloop—once disembarked you will hide somewhere. You will stay quiet a day or two like the sweet cavalier that you are—and when your good friends who wish you so well think you are tied up and have set sail for the Moroccan shore, you will reappear there like a vengeful ghost—suddenly, unexpectedly and with careful blows that you give them, they will see you are not a ghost— What do you say to that plan, my darling?

ROGER

Ah, Pousette, dear Pousette, how many obligation—how much gratitude—yes, yes, thrust I will baffle their treachery, their perfidy—Pousette, you are my savior—Pousette you are angel from the seventh heaven.

POUSETTE

As to being ethereal, it's possible but you see that in friendship. I am so light.

TOURANGEAU

O adorable Pousette—I am nestling under your wing—like a pigeon without experience.

POUSETTE

It's agreed—in a moment, the sloop—mystery! Coolness! Courage.

ROGER

And vengeance—

TOGETHER

(singing) Hide my anger
For the moment
Hide the frightful torment
Ah, when will the moment come
To punish this insolent Marquis?

TOURANGEAU and POUSETTE

(singing) Hide for the moment
All resentment
Hide the terrible torment
Soon the time will come
To punish this insolent Marquis.

(Pousette and Tourangeau leave by the left—Roger accompanies them. Sylvandire appears at the right wearing a white veil. Roger returns.)

ROGER

Was there ever such an odious plot!

(turning) Sylvandire—what audacity!

SYLVANDIRE

(sadly) Yes, it's me, Roger, I, who for the last eight months attempted every way but uselessly to see you again. I, who arrived this morning at Marseille—I, who ran to your hotel—but finally learning you were on this ship, rushed to come rejoin you.

ROGER

(ironically) Ah, I understand your hurry, Madame—on this ship, you've come to assure yourself of the success of your plans—you've come to see with your own eyes if everything is prepared for the charming trip you and your friend, Marquis de Royancourt have intentionally arranged for your humble servant.

SYLVANDIRE

(astonished, approaching Roger) Why are you speaking to me of Marquis de Royancourt, of a voyage?

ROGER

Oh—I agree it's a charming pleasure trip that your accomplice conceived—and in time an excellent way of extending indefinitely a certain meeting—indeed! To expect a jealous husband! To put between a sword one does not wish to draw and that of one's adversary a distance of several hundred leagues—! Now that, from my soul, is a tactic worthy of an honest gentleman—you still don't understand, right, Madame?

SYLVANDIRE

No, sir, no, I swear to you—oh, you are really very cruel, Roger! Or you are stupid, or you are recounting all these fables to me to avoid listening to me seriously—O my God I've really suffered enough—since the time I became your wife.

ROGER

(struck) What language! Tears!

SYLVANDIRE

Alas! I don't know what remains for me still—but explain yourself, Roger—why do you flee me—why do you always refuse to listen to me—what have I don't to you—you think me guilty?

ROGER

(heavily) Guilty! Yes, I think you're guilty.

SYLVANDIRE

If I am—it's of loving you, too much.

ROGER

You love me!

SYLVANDIRE

(very animated) Ah, more than my life, Roger—aren't you my only recourse the only friend I can hope for now in this world—my true spouse?

ROGER

Stop claiming the title of spouse, Madame, you obtained it only through the most odious trickery and you defamed it by forgetting your duties.

SYLVANDIRE

My! Great God! Ah, that's too much injustice and cruelty—this marriage that you reproach me for as a fraud—did I provoke it? Poor pensionnaire, leaving the protection of a convent, could I suspect that a father's avarice and the plans of two wretches would create it without your consent and in an odious expectation?

ROGER

What are you saying, Sylvandire? Eh, what! Finard, Royancourt—you were not their accomplice?

SYLVANDIRE

Me! Me! Ah, say their victim, Roger—and be sure it required a lot of courage to escape so many snares so marvelously constructed.

ROGER

Why no, why no—it's impossible—you deceived me—you are deceiving me still—this imprisonment in the Bastille.

SYLVANDIRE

Was the work of a monster who wanted to take me away from you. How many times did I present myself at the gates of the Bastille—well, they were shut against me by your order—always, always. I no longer had an assured asylum near my father—he was on his deathbed—at his home, Finard and my persecutor commanded as masters—I sought refuge in a holy house where I was raised—there I learned of your deliverance but at the same time you had left for Marseille. My heart guessed everything—I rushed on your trail and I've come to tell you.

(singing) Ah, I've wept so much so far from you.

Take pity on my long suffering Roger—I am coming to die near a spouse or demand vengeance, Cruel! Could you blame such a pure and tender devotion—? Weak, innocent, they wanted to oppress me— Ah, I need your heart to love me and your arm to protect me.

ROGER

Ah, if you lied with those eyes, with that voice, with those tears, no that would be too infamous! Sylvandire—dear Sylvandire, it's up to me to ask your pardon, for having mistaken you, for having outraged you for such a long time.

(sings) I curse my fatal error. Today forget my weakness. This moment, make me happy—my repenting equals my tenderness—these rights you come to claim—ah, I'm proud to give them to you. So long as you live, my heart will know how to love you—and my arm will know how to protect you.

(spoken) My Sylvandire—will you pardon me?

SYLVANDIRE

Oh, Roger! Roger! I forget everything—for now I am really happy.

(she gives him her hand, which he kissed with transport)

(Mulei, followed by a sailor, enters from the left.)

MULEI

By Allah, my loveable guests, I am happy to find you reunited aboard my ship.

(low to sailor) Everybody at his post.

SAILOR

(low) Yes, Captain.

MULEI

(to himself) Marvelous—

(Sound of a clock announcing the ships departure.)

TOURANGEAU

(entering, completely disordered and stumbling) Well, what's this, Turk?—your house is moving—we are floating—we are floating.

SYLVANDIRE

Indeed, we are moving away from the shore.

ROGER

(to Mulei) Captain, what is happening?

MULEI

(gaily) Nothing but very natural, the wind is favorable. I was only waiting for it to raise the anchor and I was unable to decide to part myself from such good company—the opportunity was too beautiful—it's a little razzia of Christians!

ROGER

And you think we will let you consummate such an infamy?

SYLVANDIRE

(stopping him) Roger—in the name of heaven.

MULEI

(smiling and using his megaphone) High seas! Wind to the rear! Keep off!

POUSETTE

(running in with the women guests) Musselman! Musselman! No stupidities, I am playing tonight. I am posted.

MULEI

(laughing) The Bey of Tunis will pay your fine—beautiful Pousette.

(Finard followed by men in uniforms enters from the right.)

CHORUS OF SAILORS

(singing) Far from the shore—
Come on, courage.
Let's voyage
And let's leave.

CHORUS OF THE OTHER CHARACTERS

Terrible slavery.
What, far from the shore
We are voyaging and leaving!

FINARD

(still enveloped in his cloak and very frightened) Captain, Captain, why, the vessel's moving. They are keeping me here despite myself! Give some orders!

MULEI

Eh! By the prophet, I'd forgotten you, my dear go-between.

ROGER

(recognizing Finard) Why, it's him—Finard! The infamous. Ah—the wretch—you will pay for everything.

(draws his sword and rushes on Finard)

MULEI

(his scimitar in hand) Chevalier, no violence, if you please.

ROGER

I have to avenge myself for his machinations against the most beautiful of women.

(d'Herbigny, as a naval officer with his arm in a scarf followed by several French naval officers.)

D'HERBIGNY

Yes, the most virtuous of women; I guarantee it.

ROGER, POUSETTE, SYLVANDIRE, & TOURANGEAU

D'Herbigny.

D'HERBIGNY

Pardon, Mr. Corsair—I've come to disturb your expedition a little—I have my frigate all prepared to bar your passage.

MULEI

(aside) Ah—the Devil.

POUSETTE

Right! But you are wounded, Vicomte?

D'HERBIGNY

Oh—a little scratch in the manner of our friend, the Marquis de Royancourt.

ROGER

Explain yourself.

D'HERBIGNY

Just now, arriving in Marseille, where I came to rejoin my ship, I met the Marquis at the gate of the city. Getting down from my chair to confront the Marquis and reproach him for his perfidies on behalf of our dear Anguilhem, was for me an affair of a moment. Forced to take his sword in his hand, after having wounded me slightly, he soon received the punishment he deserved.

ROGER

My brave d'Herbigny.

D'HERBIGNY

That's not all—he confessed to his treachery towards Madame whose innocence he proclaimed. And I ran here to prevent the execution of his final conspiracy. God be praised, I arrived in time.

ROGER

Excellent friend.

D'HERBIGNY

Come on, Mr. Corsair—your sloops into the sea—and very quickly escort your lovable guests to land.

POUSETTE

(to Mulei, who is enraged) Don't be desolate, Turk—my friend—we will leave you Mr. Finard.

FINARD

Great God!

MULEI

Pretty compensation! What do you expect me to do with this?

ROGER

By God—a mute.

POUSETTE

A superb guardian for a harem!

FINARD

(terrified) Guardian for a harem—Mercy! Why I am shaking—why they will make me put up bail—

POUSETTE

(laughing) Bon voyage, my darling!

FINAL CHORUS

They're going to leave—unhappy day for them—no more slavery.
They're going alas, to leave these parts.
He must escort them to the shore.
Unlucky day.
Yes, this moment fulfills their wishes
No more slavery.

THE OTHER CHARACTERS

(singing) Come on! Let's get out of here—
What a happy fate for us—
No more slavery—

Let's leave this odious corsair—
Regain our beautiful shore—
What a happy fate—
Yes, this moment fulfills our wishes.
No more slavery.

(Roger, Sylvandire, Pousette, d'Herbigny and Tourangeau leave. Finard wants to follow then but the pirates prevent him and keep him despite his screams.)

CURTAIN

ABOUT THE AUTHOR

Frank J. Morlock has written and translated many plays since retiring from the legal profession in 1992. His translations have also appeared on Project Gutenberg, the Alexandre Dumas Père web page, Literature in the Age of Napoléon, Infinite Artistries.com, and Munsey's (formerly Blackmask). In 2006 he received an award from the North American Jules Verne Society for his translations of Verne's plays. He lives and works in México.

www.ingramcontent.com/pod-product-compliance
Lightning Source LLC
LaVergne TN
LVHW041619070426
835507LV00008B/337